Politicking in the Barrio

Politicking in the Barrio

Essays on Latino Politics in New York

ELIESER VALENTIN

WIPF & STOCK · Eugene, Oregon

POLITICKING IN THE BARRIO
Essays on Latino Politics in New York

Wipf & Stock
An Imprint of Wipf and Stock Publishers
199 W. 8th Ave., Suite 3
Eugene, OR 97401

www.wipfandstock.com

PAPERBACK ISBN: 978-1-6667-7560-0
HARDCOVER ISBN: 978-1-6667-7561-7
EBOOK ISBN: 978-1-6667-7562-4

VERSION NUMBER 01/07/26

To the Puerto Ricans—including my father,
the Rev. Angel Valentin—that paved the way for all Latinos
in New York, and to the future—Justin, Gabriel and
Benjamin Valentin—which shines bright with promise.

Contents

CONTENTS

An Excursus

Acknowledgments

No BOOK IS EVER truly written in isolation. It really does take the support and contributions of many to make the difficulty of writing possible. This book is no different. On that note, *Politicking in the Barrio* would not have been possible without the encouragement and vision of Anthony B. Pinn, a brother and mentor. He saw possible what I couldn't, and I thank him for his guidance and above all, his love for me and my family.

I owe a special thank you to my wife, Maria Luisa Pedroza-Valentin for her patience and genuine love. We have journeyed together in life now for over twenty years, and I look forward to many more decades of trekking together. To my wonderful boys—Justin, Gabriel and Benjamin—who inspire me every single day. As the dedication notes, because of them, our future shines bright with promise. My prayer is that my life—and even this book—might serve as an inspiration to you three, and that the advancement of our people becomes your passion as well, in whatever form it may take.

Special thanks are due to my brother, Dr. Benjamin Valentin, and my sister, Bethsaida Valentin Ruiz, whose companionship and love I cherish—thank you both! And to my dear mother, Luz Belen Valentin, whose strength and faith is a model to all who have crossed her path. My dear father, Angel Manuel Valentin, passed away three years ago, a victim of the horrible Omicron wave during the global pandemic. Every day I am left with the wonderful memories he made happen, and every day pedestrians and drivers alike, see his name on the corner of 100th Street and Third Avenue in El Barrio/East Harlem. I want to thank Council Member Diana Ayala and incoming Council Member Elsie Encarnacion for spearheading the effort to name that corner, the Rev. Angel Manuel Valentin Corner.

Samuel Cruz has been an incredibly supportive friend throughout the years, and actually suggested the title for this book. Maryanna De Bartolo and Jaime Pedroza, my in-laws, have been a source of support over the years.

Just like this book was not written in isolation, my extensive political work has been done in community. I wish to thank those that I have journeyed with, folk who have sought to improve the lives of many, including Latinos in New York and beyond: Mike Nieves, Nina Saxon, the first and only Puerto Rican Latina speaker of the New York City Council Melissa Mark-Viverito, John Ruiz, former Assemblymen Jose Rivera, Nelson Denis and Adam Clayton Powell, Howard Jordan, New York City Civil Court Judges Lisa Headley, Angel Cruz, Lumarie Maldonado-Cruz, Wanda Negron and Betty Lugo have been a pleasure to work with. Assemblywoman Yudelka Tapia, State Senator Gustavo Rivera, City Council Members Elsie Encarnacion and Carmen De La Rosa, Juan Rosa, Eddie Cuesta, Erica Gonzalez, Marlene Peralta, Maria Lizardo, Jaime Estades, Lucia Gomez, Aldrin Bonilla, JC Polanco, Dr. Carlos Vargas-Ramos, Dr. Heath Brown, Dr. Hector Cordero-Guzman, Dr. John Mollenkopf, Dr. Kaliris Yimar Salas-Ramirez, Dr. Trina Nurse, Xavier Santiago, Danilo Burgos, Ny Whitaker and the New York Democratic Lawyers Council, Steven Romalewski, Jasmin Clavasquin, Angel Audiffred, Rudy Vargas, Bishop Ray Rivera and Elvin Garcia. A special thank you is due to Ben Max who opened the doors for me to share my thoughts on Latino politics to a broad audience, while he was the editor at *Gotham Gazette*.

And a thank you to Jeanmarie Evelly, who it is a pleasure to work with at *City Limits*, a new home of sorts for my columns on Latino politics in New York. Years ago, Jaime Estades founded the Latino Leadership Institute, now housed at Columbia University's School of Social Work, with the purpose of equipping Latino and other people of color with tools to participate in the electoral and public policy process. I thank Jaime for not only being a wonderful conversation partner but for inviting me to be one of the instructors at the Institute. To the students of the Latino Leadership Institute that at different points took courses with me: Assembly Member Stefani Zinerman, City Council Member Justin Sanchez, District Leaders Jasmin Sanchez, Maria and Luis Ordoñez, NYC Bronx Parks Commissioner Anthony Perez, Jasper Diaz, Nellie Sanchez, Santa Soriano, Samelys Lopez, Michael Beltzer, and labor leaders Shaun Francois, Marvin Holland, and hundreds of other students—thank you for allowing me to share and learn from all of you. It has been a joy to work with Raul Reyes and the folk at the Caribe Democratic Club, the oldest Puerto Rican Democratic club in the nation, over the years.

Of note are media and thought leaders that have been wonderful inter-locutors. Among them I note: Errol Louis, Juan Manuel Benitez, Elizabeth Kim, Ross Barkan, Rebecca Lewis, Dana Rubenstein, Emma Fitzsimmons, Harry Siegel, Sahalie Donaldson, Jeff Coltin, Annie McDonough, Michael Benjamin, Ralph Ortega, Jesus Garcia, Victor Javier Solano and the awe-some producers at Univision NY.

Dr. Hakim Lucas, president of Virginia Union University, my new academic home, has been incredibly supportive. It has also been an honor to work with Dr. Derrick Harkins during our launch of Virginia Union's new graduate center in New York. To those in the theological guild, who, are dear friends and have been supportive over the years, and from whom I have learned so much: Orlando Espin, Bobby Rivera, Carmen Nanko-Fer-nandez, Gilberto Cavazos-Gonzalez, Jean Pierre-Ruiz, Bryan Massingale, Jeremy Cruz, Efrain Agosto Jose Irizarry, Elena Procario-Foley, Rachana Umashankar, Bishop Ray Rivera, Liz Rios, and the late Roger Haight. Fred Davie has been an incredibly supportive friend and mentor. I wish to thank the Wipf and Stock team for taking on this project. A special thank you to Matthew Wimer for his diligent work and constant prodding. To Uli Guthrie, whose thoughtful editorial guidance through the years has made me a better writer, and whose friendship I deeply cherish.

Finally, I wish to express my gratitude to the publishers who first pub-lished these essays and graciously granted permission for their reprint in this volume:

PART ONE: 2017–2020

"Latino Voters and the 2017 New York City Elections" (Gotham Gazette, March 31, 2017)

"The Future of Latino Politics in New York City" (Gotham Gazette, May 17, 2017)

"Rep. Serrano's Retirement and a Looming Rumble in the Bronx" (Gotham Gazette, March 27, 2019)

"A Closer Look at Latino Voter Participation in the 2018 Elections" (Gotham Gazette, May 24, 2019)

"2020 Primaries: Winds of Change Shifting Latino Politics in NYC" (Gotham Gazette, June 26, 2020)

PART TWO: 2021–2025

"Latinos and the 2021 NYC Mayoral Election" *(Gotham Gazette, February 17, 2021)*

"Latinos and the 2021 NYC Council Elections" *(Gotham Gazette, March 4, 2021)*

"Latinos and the 2021 Council Elections in the Bronx" *(Gotham Gazette, May 11, 2021)*

"The Latino Vote and the 2021 Bronx Borough President Race" *(Gotham Gazette, May 26, 2021)*

"Latinos and the 2021 Council Elections in Queens" *(Gotham Gazette, June 8, 2021)*

"A Big Boost for Eric Adams: Latino Voters in the 2021 Mayoral Primary" *(Gotham Gazette, August 13, 2021)*

"The Case for a Latino Lieutenant Governor" *(Gotham Gazette, August 13, 2021)*

"Latino Vote '21: A Closer Look at the 2021 Democratic Primary" *(Gotham Gazette, October 29, 2021)*

"Will Latinos Lose the First Assembly Seat They Won 84 Years Ago?" *(Gotham Gazette, November 12, 2021)*

"Redistricting and Latinos in New York" *(Gotham Gazette, February 28, 2022)*

"Latinos and the 2022 Democratic Primary" *(Gotham Gazette, March 21, 2022)*

"Road to the Lieutenant Governor's Office Runs Through the Barrios of New York" *(Gotham Gazette, June 22, 2022)*

"The Pragmatic Progressivism of Ritchie Torres" *(Gotham Gazette, April 11, 2022)*

"Latino Vote '22: 5 Assembly Primaries to Watch" *(Gotham Gazette, June 26, 2022)*

"The Forgotten History of Latino Politics in New York" *(Gotham Gazette, July 25, 2022)*

"The Forgotten History of Latino Politics in New York: Part II" *(Gotham Gazette, September 9, 2022)*

"Latinos and the August 2022 New York State Senate Primary" *(Gotham Gazette, August 31, 2022)*

"Latinos, Hochul, and the 2022 Election for New York Governor" *(Gotham Gazette, October 27, 2022)*

"A Sad Day for Latinos in New York: Hector LaSalle's Rejection" *(Gotham Gazette, January 19, 2023)*

"New York Latino Politics Beyond New York City" *(Gotham Gazette, February 22, 2023)*

"A Closer Look at 2022 Gubernatorial Election Results Shows Why New York Democrats Must Pay Better Attention to Latino Voters" *(Gotham Gazette, June 1, 2023)*

"Is the Future Now for Latinos in New York Politics?" *(City Limits, October 19, 2023)*

"Latoya Joyner's Open Seat and the Importance of the Latino Vote" *(City Limits, January 16, 2024)*

"Latino Voters Can Play Key Role in the Outcome of New York's Most Contested Primary Race" *(City Limits, June 24, 2024)*

"Latinos in New York and the 2024 Presidential Election" *(City and State, December 22, 2024)*

"A New Rumble in the Bronx: Battle for the Borough Presidency" *(City Limits, May 15, 2025)*

"Latino Vote 2025: City Council Races to Watch" *(City Limits, June 17, 2025)*

"Latino Voters and the Political Earthquake in New York" *(City Limits, July 2, 2025)*

"What We Can Learn From the First Poll of Latino Voters in NYC's Mayoral Race *(City Limits, October 15, 2025)*

AN EXCURSUS

"Debunking Myths About the Latino Vote Involves Examining Religious Ideologies" *(National Catholic Reporter, January 3, 2023)*

"Moving Beyond Babylon: Latino/a Evangelicalism and Pentecostalism's Struggle for Ecclesial and Political Liberation" *(Political Theology Network, July 1, 2021)*

Introduction

THIS BOOK OFFERS AN episodic view of Latino politics in New York from 2017 to 2025—a period of both dramatic political flux and unprecedented Latino demographic growth. It is episodic in that the book's story derives from previously published thought pieces, in addition to some new material, of the elections, political figures, and social contexts of Latino politics in the largest city in the nation. While firmly rooted in Gotham's unique political ecosystem, the analysis nevertheless sheds crucial light on the broader dynamics shaping Latino political life across the United States. For New York City presents a paradox that is echoed nationally: Latinos are now the largest ethnic voting bloc in the city, surpassing both African Americans and whites in raw registration numbers. Yet this demographic prominence has not necessarily translated into proportional political power. Furthermore, the forces of gentrification, redistricting, intra-ethnic divisions, and chronically low voter turnout all threaten Latino representation—not only in East Harlem and Bushwick, but also in cities like Los Angeles, Chicago, Houston, and Miami. The reader may therefore ask: Why a book on Latino politics in New York? The response to this query will demand an explanation of each of those words: *Latino. Politics. New York.*

THE "LATINO" IN LATINO POLITICS IN NEW YORK

"Latino"—The first term in this phrase "Latino politics in New York"—refers not only to one of the fastest growing ethnic groups in New York, but in fact to the largest ethnic group in the whole state of New York. By virtue of these statistics, a treatment of Latino politics is necessary to understand the politics of and policy coming from Latino communities, and to understand how policies affect Latinos in New York more broadly. In short, the present volume is long overdue. Now, who are Latinos? And more specifically, who are Latinos in New York?

Generally speaking, *Latino*[1] is an umbrella term used to designate those in the United States who trace their backgrounds to Latin America—either through direct im/migration or through birthright. The unity despite diversity that the term Latino intends to capture should result in the understanding that *Latino* does not point to homogeneity. It is almost a cliché now to say that Latinos are not monolithic. And certainly, there is truth to this. Latinos come from a variety of Latin American countries, with differences in culture, language, accents, and the like. The difficulties inherent in the establishment of a term like *Latino* have led some to erroneously speak of *Latinidad* as a myth. Yet problematizing *Latinidad* as myth dismisses the reality that despite the many differences that exist, there is a sense of common identity based on the historical origins of our people ("1492" and the violent and unequal encounter of Europe with the Americas); based on common experiences within the nation, and based on a sense of connection to a region (Latin America). This idea of *Latinidad* is indeed quite "complex and contradictory, involving issues of immigration, colonialism, conquest, race, color, gender, sexuality, class, and language."[2] And yet, its ubiquitousness exists—from the thumping sounds of the latest Bad Bunny song, to the smells of *cuchifritos* and tacos in the *barrios*, to the growing media attention on "the Latino vote."

Latino has also been the product of a broader political project—one initiated by forces external to Latinos, and also one that many Latinos have themselves embraced. That is to say, the term Latino is a creation that moves beyond a sociological and racial category. There were practical political purposes for the creation of the term; I'll say more about this later. With respect to the forces external to Latinos, historian Benjamin Francis-Fallon has noted that "scores of influential journalists, civil rights advocates, and

1. I have always used the term "Latino" to refer more broadly to people of Latin American backgrounds in the US. In this sense I follow the work of Felipe Hinojosa, Maggie Elmore, and Sergio Gonzalez who use "Latina" or Latino" only when referring to specific gendered situations. The need for us Latinos to offer explanations on what to name ourselves points to the identity issues and crises that Latinos must endure in the US. It seems that since the early growth of Latinos in the mid-twentieth century, various terms have been used to identity Latinos, from "Spanish-speaking" to "Hispanics" to the more recent "Latinos," "Latinx," "Latin@s," and "Latine."

2. Beltran, *Trouble with Unity*, 5.

political professionals have. . .imagined a people poised to transform the country."[3] During the twentieth century these journalists and so forth wanted not only to comprehend the significance of the rise of Latinos in US life in general but to decipher the implications of this rise within the politics of the country. Surely, there was (and continues to be) an appeal to things Latino—both in cultural and political life.

Some Latinos, hoping they could get the long-due recognition they deserved, embraced the idea of a pan-Latino identity. Perhaps, finally, the once disparate Latino groups, separated not only by country of origin but by US geography (generally speaking Mexicans in the Southwest and West, Cubans in the Southeast and Puerto Ricans in the Northeast), could together gain the empowerment they could not get on their own. *Latino* thus points not only to a social and cultural reality but deliberately signals a political agenda as well. Francis-Fallon put it this way:

> Beginning roughly in 1960, a collection of political actors—from grassroots activists to US presidents—labored to mold all "Spanish-speaking Americans" (as they often denoted themselves)—irrespective of national origin, immigration status, skin color, or even language—into a single US minority group and political constituency. These architects of Latino politics defined this pan-ethnic group's public identity on the middle ground between traditional assimilation and the race-and class-conscious nationalisms of Chicano, Puerto Rican and Cuban movements.[4]

There is no longer a debate about whether to identify as a racial and ethnic bloc all those who trace their origins to Latin America. For all practical purposes, *the* Latino has been identified and defined in the US. And we are here, and continue to grow—rapidly—in number.[5]

---

3. Francis-Fallon, *Rise of the Latino Vote*, 4.

4. Francis-Fallon, *Rise of the Latino Vote*, 4.

5. The current migrant crisis unfolding in the US will only add to the increasing number of those classified as Latinos in the US. Most of these new migrants are of Venezuelan descent, and as a result of policy decisions by the likes of Governor DeSantis of Florida and Governor Greg Abbott of Texas, who have called for busing migrants to urban centers like New York and Chicago, the Venezuelan population in the US will extend beyond places like Miami, where they have had a presence for some years.

WHAT ABOUT LATINOS IN NEW YORK?

Latino communities in New York are now quite diverse. It wasn't always this way, particularly for most of the twentieth century. The very first Latino presence in New York dates back to 1613 when Juan Rodrigues, a native of the Dominican Republic (then a Spanish colony) arrived in Manhattan. His arrival did not result in a growth of Latin Americans in New York. That only really began to take shape in the late nineteenth century, with Cubans establishing an initial presence in the city. Around this time, a small contingent of Puerto Ricans began to arrive in Gotham, and interestingly enough, many Cubans and Puerto Ricans united with the purpose of fighting for Cuba independence. Only after 1917 did Puerto Ricans begin to arrive in large numbers, eventually growing to over one million by the end of the century. (Gabriel Haslip-Viera has written an excellent and succinct history of the Latino presence in New York.[6])

In the latter part of the twentieth and on into the twenty-first centuries, the Latino presence shifted palpably, first with the explosion of the Dominican population, and then of the Mexican, Ecuadorian, and Colombian communities. Indeed, one need only look at New York to understand the notion that Latinos are not homogenous. According to the latest census figures, there are approximately 3.6 million Latinos in New York, comprising 24 percent of the overall population. The National Association of Latino Elected and Appointed Officials (NALEO) has observed that the Latino population in New York grew by 15.5 percent between 2010 and 2020, from 3.4 million in 2010 to 3.9 million in 2020.[7] At the statewide level, Puerto Ricans remain the largest group among Latinos, though if current trends continue Dominicans will surpass Puerto Ricans as the largest group statewide by the next census in 2030. Within the City of New York, Dominicans have surpassed Puerto Ricans as the largest Latino group.

The Mexican population is third among Latinos, and South Americans are fourth. Ecuadorians and Colombians overwhelmingly comprise the largest share of South Americans.

These demographic realities among Latinos in the state of New York are similar to what is happening in the City of New York, except that, as mentioned above, Dominicans are now the largest Latino group. Puerto Ricans are a close second, coming in about 40,000 below Dominicans.

6. See his chapter in *Latinos in New York*.
7. NALEO Education Fund, "2020 Census Profile New York."

Census data indicates that Latinos now number almost 2.4 million in Gotham, comprising over 29 percent of the overall population. Interestingly, though the Latino population continues to grow, the Asian community is now growing at a faster pace.

The plurality of Latinos in New York City live in the borough of the Bronx, which remains the only Latino-majority borough. Queens is now the borough with the second highest number of Latinos, a significant shift since for a number of decades Manhattan had held that honor.

In short, not only are Latinos present in New York, comprising close to a third of the entire population, but Latinos are here to stay. Yet the population increase among Latinos has not resulted in political representation that reflects that growth. Nor has it resulted in improvements in Latinos' poverty levels. As we shall see later in this book, economic status can and does influence a group's likelihood of participating in the electoral process. Latinos are the poorest ethnic group in New York City, with one-fifth of all Latinos living on the poverty line.

With Latinos experiencing the highest poverty rates in the city, it is not coincidental, then, that the poorest borough in the city is the one that is majority-Latino. In fact, the 15th congressional district in the Bronx has for the past few decades been among the poorest congressional districts in the entire country. Among Latinos, Puerto Ricans have the highest poverty rate.[8] This economic reality reflects the national trend: Latinos and Blacks are on the lowest levels of the economic ladder. Of course, these economic realities lead to other elements that are often found among the poorest groups—lack of quality healthcare, high unemployment rates, many workers that are paid the minimum wage, inadequate housing conditions, high homelessness rates, poor educational standards, and high crime rates. Many Latino neighborhoods across the city are experiencing these conditions, especially Latinos in the borough of the Bronx. Ironically, the Bronx, as a result of its high Latino population, is also the place with the largest number of Latino elected officials.

My mention of these social conditions is not merely for the purpose of explicating the social realities of Latinos: it is also to point out that Latino politics does not take place in a vacuum. There is a social reality—one plagued by deep social ills—in which Latino politics is immersed, and this has wide implications for how we interpret the Latino political *realidad*.

---

8. I refer the reader to the excellent study by the Center of Latin American, Caribbean and Latino Studies at the City University of New York.

And this reality is one with which those in the political arena (particularly Latino elected officials) must and should contend. As I have written elsewhere:

> Those who serve and work in Latino politics must bear in mind the existential plight that Latinos face as a people . . . The political process for Latinos should not exclusively result in the attainment of power for the sake of power and privilege but must serve this greater good—to correct the ills that historically have plagued and made victims of Latinos. Latino politics should and must be the vehicle that can: lead to a greater valuation of our culture, serve to eliminate overt ethnic and racial bigotry, and speak to and against the despicable economic exploitation and disparity inherent in our society.[9]

THE "POLITICS" IN LATINO POLITICS IN NEW YORK

With that charge I pivot to the second word of interest: politics. It should come as no surprise that it is within the world of *politics* that communities and lives are directly affected by the many policy decisions made by policy makers, and by political executives like governors and mayors. Politics is largely about power. By power I refer to the ability of structures (and individuals within these structures) to have influence over the lives of others. Here I follow the late political theorist Robert Dahl, who understood power to mean that, "A has power over B to the extent that he can get B to do something that B would not otherwise do."[10] Others have expanded on Dahl's notion of power and have developed a variety of perspectives on politics as power, among them Michel Foucault's treatment on the subject. Dahl's theory of power remains quite practical for my purposes as it accurately portrays the nature of politics today. Following this Dahlian perspective is John Mearsheimer's explication of power regarding the nature of politics today. He writes that

> at a more practical level, politics in any society is all about competing for control of the governing institutions. Here is where power, which is based on resources like money, social capital, and access to media, matters. The more powerful a person or faction, the more likely it is to prevail in the political arena, which will then

9. Valentín, "Latino/a Religion and Politics," 462.
10. Dahl, " Concept of Power."

allow it to shape the society's political institutions in ways that en-
hance its own interests and power. In other words, the mighty get
to determine, in Harold Lasswell's famous words, "who gets what,
when and how."[11]

Following this line of thinking on politics and power, I wonder: How
have Latinos fared, particularly as a historically disenfranchised community, within the broader political arena? Has the slow but steady increase
in Latino political representation meant greater power, not just over the
constituency Latino politicians represent, but also within the wider political structures that exert power over others? And has greater Latino representation meant the possibilities of gaining access to the "resources" to
which Mearsheimer alludes, for surely, as he asserts, access to resources
often results in the type of power that helps to shape political institutions?
More than a brief response to these queries is beyond the scope of this
book. Based on the conditions Latinos endure, to which I have briefly alluded above, the answer to the questions above must be a resounding no:
the slow but steady rise in Latino representation has not resulted in conditions that ameliorate the Latino *realidad*. To be sure, Latino elected and
appointed officials are not solely at fault. Latinos, like other minoritized
leaders, have had to contend with a political system that continues to see
them as inferior. This does not excuse the immoral behavior of some Latinos that have taken advantage of certain power (as slight as it may be) for
their own personal goals and interests. Latino elected officials, specifically,
must contend with the fact that the dire economic and social conditions
of their constituents often means that their access to the resources read-
ily available to the dominant group eludes them. One need only examine
campaign finance filings to see that Latino political candidates and elected
officials do not raise money at the levels their White counterparts do. The
obscene amounts of money required to run for higher political office means
it is much more difficult for Latinos to compete. As Mearsheimer has noted,
the powerless (which often means those without "resources") cannot pre-
vail in a system that requires significant resources.

Realizing that the electoral system requires more parity across racial
and economic lines, New York City introduced a new campaign finance
system some decades ago with the purposes of "leveling the playing field" so
that more candidates could have greater abilities to seek elected office. This
new system would allow for the possibility, they asserted, for minoritized

11. Mearsheimer, *Great Delusion*, 39.

individuals to compete for elected positions across the city. Moreover, the new campaign finance system would seek to prevent corporations and big funders from exerting too much influence on the city's political process. Contribution limits were set, and corporate money was prohibited. By following these rules, so the thought went, candidates would be rewarded by receiving public funding. Currently, candidates abiding by these campaign finance rules are awarded $8 in public money for every $1 raised. Nevertheless, this system, which has been deemed a model for other municipalities in the country, has not always worked favorably for people of color. Take the situation of Fernando Ferrer in 2005, the first Latino to win the nomination of a major party for the mayoralty in New York City. Despite being part of this generous campaign finance system (at the time of his candidacy candidates received $4 for every $1 raised), Ferrer was vastly outspent by the incumbent and billionaire mayor, Michael Bloomberg. Bloomberg spent upwards of $100 million to win re-election. This is just one example of the powerlessness even of those that are already part of the political system, as was Ferrer, the then Bronx borough president.

As this shows, the politics to which I refer here and throughout this book focuses mostly on the nature of electoral and governmental politics. I realize that politics can and does have a much broader significance and definition. I have previously defined politics with an eye toward this broader view, seeing it as involving "the structural (governmental and otherwise), the *responses* to the structural by the greater public (by means of voting participation and mobilization, advocacy work, and so forth), and the *inherent relationships* between all in the public sphere."[12] Yet, because our political system and current context have placed a greater emphasis on the power exerted by government (making the electoral process an important vehicle toward the attainment of that power), I have chosen to focus on the electoral and policy realities that are evident within Latino communities in New York.

The strategic focus on representation and elections in electoral politics that I take in this book unfortunately minimizes examination of community organizations and its leaders within the development of Latino politics in New York. This has been a strategic choice, one not intended to minimize the important role that community organizations have historically played in the continuing development of Latino politics in New York. Indeed, I believe that many organizations—like the critical advocacy

12. Valentin, *Latino/a Religion and Politics*, 456.

work of ASPIRA (meaning *aspire*) and the work of Antonia Pantoja—were pivotal in the development of Latino leaders. Indeed, the advancement of Latino politics—particularly as it relates to increasing political representation and participation at the electoral and advocacy realms—would not have been possible without the critical role that community organizations and its leaders played.

Jose E. Cruz, a Latino political scientist, has made a clear distinction between electoral political dynamics and community-based organizational work. As one of the few thinkers who have reflected on varying aspects of Latino politics in New York,[13] Cruz has proposed that electoral political work and community organizational actions are part and parcel of *Latino politics* more broadly. He has defined the electoral work undertaken by Latinos in New York as an "elite-level" reality, one that is distinct from the community-level work that community organizations do. Cruz has written two books, one focusing on each of the distinctions he has made with respect to Latino politics.[14]

THE "NEW YORK" IN LATINO POLITICS IN NEW YORK

Historically, New York has been a hub for many generations of migrants from all over the world. We can point to the arrival of Germans and Irish in the nineteenth century, and Italians in the late nineteenth and early twentieth centuries as prime examples. Back then, migrants understood New York as a place that welcomed migrants, a place that offered a wealth of

13. The corpus of work in Latino politics in the US is growing. Clearly, the rise of the Latino population and the recent increase in Latino political representation (Congress now has the largest class of Latino elected officials in the history of the US) has created the need to think through the implications of this rise to Latino communities, and to the wider US body politic. Yet, academic and popular writings reflecting on Latino politics in New York remain scarce. In addition to Cruz, another of the few thinkers who did reflect, write, and work extensively on the idea of a Latino politics in New York, was Angelo Falcon. Falcon was the founder of the National Institute of Latino Policy, a New York-based think tank. Jose Ramon Sanchez likewise wrote a critical work on Puerto Rican politics in New York.

14. Both of Cruz's books are limited to the work of Puerto Ricans in New York between 1960 and 1990. The importance of highlighting the work of Puerto Ricans in the development of Latino politics in New York is critical. This book you are reading does not limit the scope of Latino politics in New York to the work of Puerto Ricans, nor does it limit itself to a specific time period as part of the broader nature of the work. I believe that any interpretation of Latino politics in New York must take into account its broad history, development, and existing realities.

opportunities for their advancement. Of course, migrants often encountered a quite different reality—scorn from those already there, substandard housing conditions, and low-paying jobs. Nevertheless, many thrived. A number of Latino groups began arriving to New York City in the latter part of the nineteenth century. They were mostly Cubans and Puerto Ricans, though the Cuban population was larger back then. New York City became a hub for many Cubans that were part of the Cuban liberation movement, one that sought to break free from Spanish domination. Interestingly enough, some Puerto Ricans arrived in New York to assist some of the Cubans in their efforts. The early presence of Latinos was one of collaboration and mutual support in the largest metropolis in the nation.

Within the first few decades of the twentieth century, Puerto Ricans became the largest Latino group in New York. After what is now called "The Great Migration" in the 1950s, Puerto Ricans surpassed the one million mark in Gotham City alone.[15] As a result of the large Latino population, New York City became a central location for the rise of Latino politics, and its mark would be felt nationally. Since the election of Herman Badillo to the US Congress, Latino political leaders in New York have become central figures in the development of Latino politics in the US. No discussion of Latino politics is possible without considering Latinos from New York. Thus, the content of this book has import not just for New York politics but also for politics more broadly.

A NOTE ON METHODOLOGY

While this book hopes to reach an informed general audience, because it also seeks to engage those who interpret politics from the perspectives of the social sciences and humanities I want to say a word about my methodological approach. I use several methods of inquiry to interpret the Latino political reality I describe. On one hand, I use historical analysis to help us understand how Latinos have arrived at this juncture. Clearly, events and movements do not happen *ex nihilo*; there are prior events, people and movements that have helped shaped the arrival of current contextual situations. For example, the increase in Dominican, Colombian, and Ecuadorian political representation in New York could not have happened without the pioneering work of Puerto Ricans, whose arrival over a century ago

15. The essays on the "The Forgotten History of Latino Politics in New York" examines some of this history in more detail.

helped pave the way for newer Latino groups to gain political representation within a system that remains hostile to minoritized groups like Latinos.

Historical analysis can also lead to the development of theoretical postulations that discern not just the current moment but can also infer future possibilities. For instance, the late historian Arthur Schlesinger, following the work of his own father, advanced a cyclical theory of political history. He perceived fluctuating patterns in US American political history—ideological shifts between liberalism and conservatism. Major ideological shifts, Schlesinger posited, were discernible every thirty years or so.[16] Because Latino New Yorkers have consistently supported Democratic candidates, ideological realignments are harder to track, but other cycles are visible. First, Latino political standing oscillates from marginalization to centrality and back to partial disempowerment. Second, institutional incorporation rises and recedes as representatives gain influence and then encounter retrenchment with party realignments. These cycles are shaped—though not caused—by intra-Latino demographic reconfiguration (nativity, generation, national-origin mix, class, neighborhood). I elaborate these patterns in later chapters through an adapted Schlesinger framework, which treats recurring liberal–conservative eras (roughly every three decades) as a heuristic while shifting the analytic focus beyond ideology.

A more common methodological approach to Latino politics is one that uses social scientific research methods. Several methodologies are quite effective at capturing patterns in Latino voting participation, and survey research is a proven method for understanding Latino vote and issue preferences and the like. In my own work, several proven techniques have been particularly helpful in understanding Latino voting patterns in New York. Political scientist Matt Barreto has been quite helpful in describing one of these—ecological inference.[17] Ecological inference uses aggregate information to ascertain individual-level information. Barreto and others have noted that although this method has not always proved helpful in certain fields, ecological inference is especially useful for ascertaining Latino voting preference and patterns, specifically Latino voting (individual-level data) within specific precincts (aggregate data). In a later chapter, I apply

16. Schlesinger's cyclical theory of political history can be found in his text, *Cycles of American History*.

17. For more on the use of ecological inference for examining Latino voting realities, see the excellent article, "eiCompare."

this method to some of the data to understand recent Latino voting patterns at the city and state levels.

I use both historical and social scientific methods to reflect on Latino political realities in New York. Contrary to some academic "purists," I do not believe that the exclusive use of particular method of inquiry suffices when examining Latino politics. In order to capture the diverse reality that is anything Latino (particularly politics), I have found employing various methods to be pivotal and necessary.

OUTLINE OF THE BOOK

This book and its story is arranged chronologically, by date of publication, and has two parts. Part one covers the years 2017 to 2020. This is a period of shifts. On one hand, we see growth in the number of Latinas in elected office. We also observe a certain changing of the guard—a growing number of younger Latinos are elected into political office, including the shocking victory of Alexandria Ocasio-Cortez in 2018 and the election of Ritchie Torres to Congress in 2020. Torres replaced the long-time Congressman, Jose Serrano. This period also reflected a growing attention to what we now refer as the "Latino vote." This greater attention led to some increases in Latino voting participation. But as I point out, the increase in participation was short lived. And to add to the challenges of this 2017–2020 period, some Latino neighborhoods continued to grapple with increased gentrification and the threat of political representation.

Part two covers the years 2021 to 2025. This period reflects the ebb and flow that has become the reality of Latino political life over the last half decade. On one hand, Latinos were a pivotal part of the Eric Adams mayoral victory in 2021, and the Zohran Mamdani victory in 2025. We can also say that Governor Kathy Hochul's victory in 2022 was in part achieved thanks to substantial Latino support. In fact, Hochul went on to appoint Antonio Delgado as lieutenant governor in a nod to the growing force of Latinos in New York. She, along with the rest of New York, would go on to learn that Delgado was not, in fact, Latino.

However, this period saw a steady decline in Latino voting participation. The decline took place amidst a global pandemic, heightened poverty, higher crime in Latino neighborhoods, and a lack of cohesion in Latino political leadership.

The book ends with an excursus containing two essays that examine the role of religion in Latino political life. The essay *"Debunking myths about Latino vote involves examining religious ideologies"* explores how certain ideological leanings affect voting behavior. For instance, Latino Catholics and Latino Evangelicals have tended to diverge in candidate and party preferences. The second essay, *"Moving Beyond Babylon: Latino/a Evangelicalism and Pentecostalism's Struggle for Ecclesial and Political Liberation"* was one of the first to examine the role of Christian Nationalism within Latino Evangelicalism.

As you read this book, I hope that my love for my people is evident throughout the stories I tell. My life's work has essentially been to give voice to an often-voiceless people. My desire has been to inspire and prod our folk to aspire to greater and proper representation at all levels, with the purpose of helping to improve the lives of all who name themselves Latinos—whether they come from the Caribbean, South or Central or North America.

PART ONE

2017–2020

1

Latino Voters and the 2017 New York City Elections

FOR THE FIRST TIME in history, there are more Latino voters in New York City than African Americans. In fact, Latinos now account for 23% (977,514) of all registered voters in NYC (4,281,946) and they are a quarter (735,641) of all registered Democrats (2,942,337), according to data from Prime New York's voter analysis.

As the largest ethnic group in the city—and the entire United States— the Latino presence in New York is palpable: from the store-front taquerias and *cuchifritos*, to the salsa and merengue beat in the streets, to the baseball and soccer stars that dominate our airwaves.

This presence has also been felt electorally, but, until now, the Latino voting explosion has not increased their political representation. In fact, Latino-majority districts are now under direct threat from the drawing of specific districts, and the gentrification of traditionally Latino neighbor-hoods such as El Barrio (East Harlem) and Loisaida (the Lower East Side).

In Loisaida, the 2nd Council District has been represented by a Latino/a for almost thirty years. Though currently represented by Rosie Mendez, real estate development and gentrification has created a spike of younger white voters—who now outnumber Latinos by over 12,000 regis-tered voters.

Other city districts do not face this direct threat to Latino political representation, but if the current demographic dynamics continue, it will become a widening reality. Districts that have experienced a drastic shift include the 38th Council District, currently represented by Carlos Menchaca. On a larger scale the 7th Congressional District, which contains some of the 38th Council District, is showing this same influx of younger white voters, and many of them are not familiar with the incumbent Rep. Nydia Velazquez.

In spite of these electoral changes, the impact of Latinos cannot be ignored by future candidates, incumbents, or anyone. Some recent elections make this point, and very dramatically. The last time a Latino topped the ticket in a municipal election was in 2005, when Fernando Ferrer won the mayoral Democratic primary. In that election, Latinos already constituted a quarter of the entire Democratic electorate, and over 90,000 Latinos voted in the primary. In 2013, the year in which Mayor de Blasio won his election, we saw a decline in the percentage of Latinos voting, but an actual increase in the actual number of Latinos who turned out. The increase totaled over 20,000 new voters, for a total of over 111,000 Latino votes in 2013. This increase occurred despite the absence of any Latino citywide candidate in that year. (Data based on Prime New York data and my own analysis.)

Current efforts to register more Latinos to vote and the rise of younger and active Latino community leaders will undoubtedly lead to greater Latino voter participation. My own statistical modeling and data analysis shows as many as 40,000 additional Latinos potentially voting in the upcoming 2017 New York City primary. Any candidate who ignores this powerhouse voting bloc—from the mayor on down—will do so at their peril.

In 2017 every candidate must be aware of, and sensitive to, the issues that affect Latinos in New York. Those issues can no longer be taken for granted. As a dominant citywide voting bloc, Latinos must be placed front and center in any policy or electoral agenda. The recognition of Latino issues is not merely ethical. It is also good politics, because along with their growing electoral power, Latinos are developing a memory. They will remember who has taken them seriously, and who has not. Every elected official in New York, every current and future politician, should remember this fact.

2

The Future of Latino Politics
in New York City

Just last month the annual Somos El Futuro legislative conference took place in Albany. Over 30 years ago a group of Latino elected officials and community leaders initiated the conference as a means to highlight issues important to Latinos and to shine a light on the plight of Latinos in New York. The visionary leadership of these early pioneers was to capitalize on and give consciousness to the ever-growing presence of Latinos in the state. Perhaps the name itself, Somos El Futuro—We are the Future—was not only a testament of the current influence of the Latino presence in New York at the time but also an apt moniker of the eventual significance of this surging community.

In a recent column, I highlighted the growing Latino electoral presence in New York City. Latinos now make up almost a quarter of the entire city electorate. Based on sheer numbers Latinos can now claim that they are not just the future but that *estamos aqui ahora*—we are here now.

With this increasing presence has come a steady growth in Latino political representation, even though gentrification poses a real threat to some Latino-majority districts. The rise of the Latino presence citywide produced some noteworthy political leaders that in fact became pioneers and leading figures in our community. Among them we can note the work of Tony Mendez, Oscar Garcia Rivera, Herman Badillo, Olga Mendez, Angelo Del Toro, and Jose Rivera.

Without a doubt, these pioneers have paved the way for a newer crop of Latino political leaders, many of whom are doing excellent work in their respective communities. Many are not only providing pivotal leadership in their districts, some have the potential to be serious and credible candidates for citywide office in the near future. It's important to also note that the extremely important work of providing leadership in Latino areas—communities often riddled with rampant poverty, decrepit housing, and overcrowded schools—is not only being provided by elected officials. In fact, there are a number of Latino community activists, many of them young, fighting ardently for the justice that Latinos demand and deserve.

The last time a Latino gained a top spot on a citywide ballot was Fernando Ferrer in 2005. Prior to that it was Badillo, whose 1969 mayoral candidacy gained the affection of Latinos in New York (he also ran two more times for mayor). It is my belief that for the 2021 elections, Latinos can once again have a Latino (possibly more than one) launching a credible campaign for citywide office. The question is, who might these candidates be that can gain the attention of not only Latinos but also a wider electorate and public? Who will be the next Ferrer or Badillo?

The first that has to be highlighted is Ruben Diaz, Jr., the current Bronx Borough President. Very recently, Diaz, Jr. was a constant name in the ever-present rumor mill regarding a potential challenge to Mayor de Blasio. Diaz, Jr. instead has decided to seek re-election. Over the years, he has taken credit for a boon in Bronx development projects (something which in fact began occurring during Ferrer's tenure in the borough presidency) and has been a fierce advocate for the people in his borough. While lacking the intellectual heft of a Badillo and Ferrer, Diaz, Jr. has a magnetic personality that is sure to attract many as his final term as borough president nears an end.

There is also Melissa Mark-Viverito, the current speaker of the City Council. Her position has given her the most Latino clout in recent years to influence citywide policy, some of which she has used. This platform has provided Mark-Viverito an ample opportunity to garner broad attention and to push for policy issues pertinent to a wider public and also to Latinos in particular. However, since she is term-limited and likely will be out of the public eye on a consistent basis, her chances for a successful citywide race in four years will be virtually impossible.

One person to keep an eye on is Ritchie Torres, a Bronx City Council member. Elected in 2013, at the youthful age of 25, Torres has proven to be a solid legislator, championing important causes, and also fighting ardently for better housing conditions for public housing residents. Torres is charismatic, well liked by his peers, and whip-smart. He has the uncanny ability to probe and articulate complex policy matters. At 29 years of age, Torres will surely be one to watch for years to come and could be a formidable candidate for either Bronx borough president or the city's public advocate if he chooses to aspire to either position.

When looking at the horizon of Latino political leaders, the future seems bright—the three aforementioned names are not the only ones on the list. With the continuing rise of Latinos in the overall population and increased voting participation, it may be quite possible that New York City will soon have its first Latino mayor.

3

Rep. Serrano's Retirement and a Looming Rumble in the Bronx

IT'S TIME FOR A rumble in the Bronx. After 29 years in Congress and 44 years in elected office, Congressional Rep. José Serrano has decided to retire from office. Together with the likes of Herman Badillo, José Rivera, Robert Garcia, Gerena Valentin, and Ramon Velez in the Bronx, Serrano has been a pioneering figure within the Latino/Puerto Rican political landscape in New York City.

Serrano fought at the frontlines for Latino political representation at a time when Puerto Ricans were left out of the political equation despite their burgeoning numbers. Serrano, and the rest, fought arduously for this long-sought-after recognition. Their hard work paid off. Serrano won an Assembly seat in 1975.

While Serrano's early work to gain Latino political representation is not debatable, the rest of his legacy is more dubious. Serrano has not been known for any sort of legislative prowess. The South Bronx, which he represents, has long been a poverty stricken area that has seen scant federal resources for decades, despite Serrano's long tenure in Congress.

As a result of this record, observers like long-time political operative Mike Nieves had surmised that a formidable and credible candidate could defeat Serrano. No one ever did.

Serrano's legacy notwithstanding, the eyes of our political world will now turn to the 15th Congressional district in the Bronx to see who will succeed him in Congress. The timing of Serrano's retirement announcement coincides with City Council Member Ritchie Torres' own recent announcement that he would challenge the incumbent representative for the seat. In a previous column, I mentioned that Torres would be one to watch as we eye the future of Latino politics in the city. His intellectual abilities, grasp of public policy, and ability to articulate his view have deservedly caught people's attention.

Torres is clearly a formidable candidate for the "open" congressional seat. Most of his Council district, which he first won in 2013, lies within Serrano's Congressional district. After six years in the Council, Torres has been able to gain some recognition among voters for his work on behalf of his constituents, particularly in areas affecting NYCHA residents.

Various other names are being floated at this nascent stage. Among them are former City Council Speaker Melissa Mark-Viverito. Mark-Viverito has just come off a dismal showing in her race for the citywide position of public advocate. Yet she still holds some name recognition, particularly among Latinos. Her home congressional district is currently represented by Adriano Espaillat but since there are no in-district residency requirements for a congressional seat, she could still make a play for the Serrano seat.

Then there is Assemblymember Marcos Crespo, who is also the Bronx Democratic leader. Crespo's Assembly district lies entirely within Serrano's Congressional district and he would therefore potentially go into a race of this sort with a natural base of followers. Some will question his alliance with Council Member Ruben Diaz, Sr., who has been challenged for repeated homophobic statements and positions. But given Crespo's potential to capitalize on some of the resources that would naturally come his way by virtue of his party position, he would quickly be considered a leading candidate for the position.

Yet another recent public advocate candidate might also throw his hat in the ring. Since Michael Blake's election to the Assembly, and then his appointment to be a vice chair of the Democratic National Committee, rumors have swirled that he would one day challenge José Serrano.

That day never came. But this opening can provide an opportunity for Blake. Despite losing the public advocate race, Blake won his home borough of the Bronx and did fairly well in the portion covering Serrano's Congressional district. And if he's the only African-American in the race, that could also create a path to victory for Blake. With multiple formidable Latino candidates, a strong African-American candidate could win the seat.

Almost a third of the Democratic electorate in this Congressional district is African-American. Over 55 percent is Latino. If the race takes an ethnic path, that could lead to a split Latino vote and a more consolidated African American vote.

Then there's state Senator Gustavo Rivera. Rivera, first elected in 2010, represents a swath of Serrano's district in the state Senate. He has earned admiration from many progressives for standing up to the Bronx political machinery and for policies that progressives have long championed.

Lastly, if he were to step up, one elected official who could clear many if not all in the field would be Bronx Borough President Ruben Diaz, Jr. Diaz, Jr. is known throughout the borough and remains popular among many voters. Furthermore, this district has always been his home district— he represented parts of it in the Assembly for 13 years. Diaz Jr.'s capable communications guru, John DeSio, has tweeted that the borough president is not interested in the position. The borough president appears focused on launching a mayoral bid. But politics is practical and a congressional run could be an easier path to victory than a citywide mayoral race. All this is conjecture, of course. What's certain is that we can expect a free-for-all for the position ahead of the 2020 vote, and thus another rumble in the Bronx.

4

A Closer Look at New York City Latino Voter Participation in the 2018 Elections

NYC Votes and the Voter Assistance Advisory Committee recently released their mandated report regarding voting participation in New York City, which skyrocketed in 2018. While the report contains fascinating analyses, it does not, nor does it seek to, delve into the role that people of color, in this case specifically Latinos, played in last year's elections. But their role was definitely pivotal, and it particularly affected the New York gubernatorial primary.

According to my own analysis, over half a million more voters came out to the polls in the 2018 Democratic primaries than in the 2014 primaries. Over a million more voters voted in the 2018 general election than in the 2014 general election.

This enormous increase in voting participation was evident across all racial groups. But of them all, the increase among Latino voters in New York City was slightly greater. Compared to the 2014 primaries, when Latinos comprised 17% of the overall New York City electorate (47,592 voters), in 2018 Latinos increased their voter share to 20% of the city electorate, with 169,667 Latinos going to the polls.

In the 2018 general election Latinos also comprised 20% of the city's electorate, increasing their voter turnout by nearly 300,000 voters over the 2014 general election. Of these, 55% of the Latino vote came from two boroughs—the Bronx and Manhattan—and 42% of the Latino vote came from Brooklyn and Queens. One interesting change from previous elections is that the Latino vote in Queens has increased. In previous years, Manhattan made up almost 30% of all Latino voters but that number is now dwindling, in my estimation likely because of the decrease in Puerto Rican voters in East Harlem and the Lower East Side.

But Queens has seen a spike in Latino voting participation, with 30,000 more voters going to the polls in 2018 than in 2014. Queens Latino voters now comprise 21% of all Latino voters in the city, the largest increase in percentages of all the boroughs. In the 2018 general election, Queens residents made up a quarter of all Latino voters. The Bronx remains the borough with the most Latino voters.

Lest you think this column is painting too rosy a picture of Latino voting participation, here's the reality check: only 20% of all eligible Latino Democratic voters in New York City voted in the 2018 Democratic primary. In the 2018 general election, 37% of all eligible registered Latinos voted in New York City. In comparison, 45% of registered black voters in the city went to the polls in the general election.

To be sure, the lack of Latino voting participation in New York City is not unique to Gotham. Studies indicate that this lack of participation is prevalent nationally. This has been well documented by Bernard Fraga in his book The Turnout Gap. There, Fraga observes on the basis of careful research that Latino (along with Asian-American) voting participation lags behind all other groups nationally.

Clearly, much remains to be done when it comes to pushing for a greater electoral presence among Latinos. The question is whether its leaders, particularly Latino elected officials, have the wherewithal to make this a priority.

The most recent citywide election (the February special election for public advocate) barely turned out 10% of Latino voters. Granted, all political observers predicted that this election would be a low-turnout affair. But the abysmal turnout among Latinos should raise many questions of concern and should compel Latino leaders to strategize ways to increase voting participation. Otherwise, the "sleeping giant" moniker given to Latinos will persist.

5

Against All Odds

The Improbable Election
of Alexandria Ocasio-Cortez

2018 WAS THE YEAR of the woman. Nationally, 118 women won election to Congress, the most in the history of this country. Closer to home in New York, history was made with the election of Letitia James, who will serve as the state's attorney general.

Yet it was Alexandria Ocasio-Cortez who sent tremors through the political establishment by defeating Joe Crowley. Crowley is not only the fourth-highest-ranking Democrat in the House of Representatives but is also the powerful leader of the Queens Democratic organization.

Then 28 years old, now 29, with no political experience (aside from helping in Bernie Sanders's presidential campaign), an economics degree, and a bartending job, Ocasio-Cortez set out to do the impossible—defeat an established and powerful sitting incumbent. Statistics show that incumbents generally have a 92% re-election success rate. It's nearly impossible to defeat an incumbent, no matter what position the incumbent holds.

Most of us perceived the Alexandria Ocasio-Cortez campaign as the "little engine that could" campaign: no one gave it a chance for success. Ocasio-Cortez would have to go against all odds to pull that one off. And she did.

How she pulled it off is equally surprising. The conventional political wisdom held that in order for Ocasio-Cortez to have any glimmer of hope, she would have to defeat Crowley in heavily Latino and African American areas. After the 2002 redistricting efforts, the Crowley district reached deep into certain pockets of districts represented by people of color. Clearly, the dynamics of future Crowley victories would have to extend to areas he had never represented. That is, if anyone dared to challenge him.

Crowley's power was so vast, the thinking went, that even powerhouse names in the Bronx (large portions of the Bronx were added post-redistricting), like Ruben Diaz, Jr., opted not to challenge to the Queens Goliath. But that didn't stop Ocasio-Cortez. And in fact Ocasio-Cortez would not win in these nonwhite regions, contrary to what the political establishment had expected.

With her decision to take on Crowley out of the way, Ocasio-Cortez went straight to work, early and often knocking on doors in order to speak to voters directly. She was eager to garner as much press attention as possible, in spite of the New York City media counting her out. Ocasio-Cortez wisely sought out leftist news outlets and quickly earned attention from national progressive organizations and leaders. Surely, this attention assisted the little-engine-that-could campaign in raising much-needed cash to help the upstart campaign.

Ocasio-Cortez used social media in creative and organic ways. This allowed her to speak to a wider universe of voters, voters who normally would not be enthusiastic about voting in a June federal primary. Ocasio-Cortez's campaign understood that in order to make this a battle, she would have to try to expand the electorate and seek out a nontraditional base of voters, ones not accustomed to voting in primaries.

As the campaign wound down, and with Ocasio-Cortez earning more attention, some New York political leaders began to glance her way, albeit with some trepidation. That was evident in the almost literally last minute endorsement from Cynthia Nixon, the failed gubernatorial candidate who was taking on another political giant, Governor Andrew Cuomo.

The traditional progressive groups in New York did not even dare look at Ocasio-Cortez's campaign. The Working Families Party, which seemed to revel in her victory to the point of almost taking credit for it, in fact endorsed Crowley and not Ocasio-Cortez.

As results began to trickle in on June 26, the coalition of voters that Ocasio-Cortez's campaign hoped it had energized, came out for her in astonishing numbers. And indeed nonwhite voters did not propel her campaign to victory. Since Ocasio-Cortez is a Puerto Rican Latina, conventional wisdom had held that she could potentially do well among Latino/a voters. Once again, Ocasio-Cortez defied both the odds and conventional thinking by beating Crowley in the more white regions of the district. In fact, she either lost or came close to losing in the overwhelmingly Black and Latino areas.

For instance, Ocasio-Cortez lost in the 35th Assembly district in Queens, long a bastion of solid African American voting. She also lost the 87th Assembly district, a majority Latino district that has been represented by Puerto Rican elected officials for over two decades.

It was in the more white, gentrifying sections of Queens, like Astoria and Sunnyside, that Ocasio-Cortez proved to be formidable. And whereas there had been questions as to whether Ocasio-Cortez would be able to turn out younger voters, who historically were less inclined to vote in primary elections, in fact Ocasio-Cortez managed to increase younger voters (in the 18–39 age range) by over 12%. Indeed, these young voters composed almost a third of the entire primary vote.

As we fast forward to December 2018, the buzz in the political world is whether Ocasio-Cortez can continue to defy the odds. Will Ocasio-Cortez stand out from the rest of her 434 colleagues in the House? Can she govern effectively, or will she have to take a back seat to House leadership and those that have more seniority, which in the House has long been the name of the game?

On this too Ocasio-Cortez is again defying the odds by proposing a Green New Deal, a creative and necessary proposal to curb the consequences of a potential ecological disaster. Environmental groups are fiercely organizing and lobbying congressional leaders with the hopes of passing the Green New Deal, the audacious plan of an incoming 29-year-old Puerto Rican congresswoman. It seems that Ocasio-Cortez will continue to do what she has done in 2018, and yes, perhaps her entire life—to defy the odds.

6

Latino Politics and Gentrification

THAT GENTRIFICATION OF TRADITIONALLY Latino neighborhoods would eventually threaten Latinos' political representation has long been expected. A process that produces high end development with the aim of making neighborhoods more suitable for a higher class of people and their tastes, gentrification has political implications in addition to its more often discussed economic impact.

The first real evidence of this threat to Latino's political representation came from data about who turned out to vote in the 2018 primary season.

Take the senate seat recently won by Julia Salazar. A Latina of Colombian descent, she defeated Martin Dilan, a long-time incumbent of Puerto Rican descent. But it wasn't Latinos who propelled her to victory: it was white voters, mainly those who are part of the gentrification wave in Williamsburg and Bushwick.

While not all gentrifiers are white, U.S. Census data indicates that the overwhelming majority of those gentrifying Williamsburg and Bushwick, for instance, are white. Since the 2000 census, these two neighborhoods have seen a 126% increase in the white population. Yet it is Latinos, not white gentrifiers, who still outnumber other groups in this district. So what gives?

When mobilized, gentrifiers heavily influence the outcome of an election in a district where previously Latino voters dominated. Consider the following: Across the city, there was a substantial overall increase in voter turnout for the September 2018 Democratic primary election. According to my analysis, in the Dilan-Salazar district battle White voter participation in 2018 increased by 167% over the 2017 citywide primaries. Among that district's Democratic voters, whites comprise 23% of the electorate, Latinos almost double that, at 44%. Who turned out for that election? Whites at 32% and Latinos scarcely more at 35% of the overall vote.

There is no doubt that the gubernatorial Democratic primary, and specifically the support for Cynthia Nixon's candidacy, helped boost turnout among white voters in the Salazar district. Nixon, Governor Cuomo's primary opponent) was the preferred candidate of progressive organizations and these organizations were especially active in the Salazar district. Both Nixon and Salazar routed their opposition in the election districts overwhelmingly populated by gentrifiers.

Yet, the Salazar victory happened as much because of the lack of voting enthusiasm among Latino voters as because of the increased role of white gentrifiers in Brooklyn. Plainly stated: given the high percentage of Latinos among all registered voters, Latino voters are not turning out to vote in sufficient numbers.

This has been well documented by Bernard Fraga in his book The Turnout Gap. Fraga observes on the basis of careful research that Latino (along with Asian American) voting participation lags behind all other groups nationally. Recent elections show that poor voting participation by Latinos is the reality in New York. Gentrification exacerbates this lack of voting participation and will soon affect Latino political representation— unless we Latinos and our allies vote.

The 34th council district in Brooklyn (that overlaps with the Salazar senate district) now represented by Antonio Reynoso, could see representation changes in the next election cycle in 2021. Latinos make up 46% of all Democratic voters, far outnumbering other racial groups. The next largest group are whites, who comprise 30% of the Democratic electorate. (I restrict myself to the Democratic electorate since Democrats far outnumber all other parties and thus determine the outcome of these elections.)

Yet, in 2018, whites comprised 40% of the Democratic electorate, surpassing Latinos in raw numbers by almost 800 votes. According to my research, this is the first time since this district became predominantly Latino that Latino voters have not comprised the majority of its electorate.

Crossing the river to East Harlem—another Latino neighborhood that has seen a spike in gentrification for at least 10 years now—we see a consistent increase in voting registration and participation among white gentrifiers. In the September primary, white voters actually doubled their turnout rates from the previous election cycle. In new voter registration over the last two years, white gentrifiers have surpassed African Americans, who have been the second largest ethnic group in East Harlem for decades.

Latino political representation is not under the same threat in East Harlem as it is in the neighborhoods in Brooklyn described above. Still, at the current pace of electoral change, the ramifications of this dynamic on Latino political representation will hit us hard in the coming years.

Rather than create racial discord, my intent here is to point out another consequence of gentrification in many neighborhoods across our city. To the displacement of families and individuals of mostly poor means, and to the increase in rents and cost of living we must now add the political ramifications of such demographic shifts caused by gentrification—namely, the threat to Latino political representation.

7

2020 Primaries

Winds of Change Shifting Latino
Politics in New York City

As this month's primary election results seem to be proving, the winds of change are blowing and are shifting the direction of Latino politics in New York City. Has a new era of leadership in Latino political representation arrived?

In the Bronx, Ritchie Torres seems to be ahead with a comfortable margin, defeating Michael Blake, long-time politico Ruben Diaz, Sr., and many others in the 15th Congressional District. In these pages I predicted that Torres was one to take very seriously. The future has arrived. When all ballots are counted, I expect Torres to pull off the victory. Torres now joins Alexandria Ocasio-Cortez (AOC), Nydia Velazquez, and Adriano Espaillat as the Latino congressional representatives in New York City. Torres and AOC, though, represent a new and perhaps more progressive voice, one that is representative of the younger Latino generation. Surveys indicate that members of this younger generation tend to be more progressive than their parents and grandparents. Three years ago (when AOC was still bartending) I wrote: "Torres is charismatic, well-liked by his peers, and whipsmart. He has the uncanny ability to probe and articulate complex policy matters. At 29 years of age, Torres will surely be one to watch for years to come."

Now with a bigger platform, I anticipate that Torres will be a formidable force on behalf of the Latino community for years to come.

Perhaps the strongest wind of change in Latino politics is blowing from Queens. Jessica González-Rojas appears to be defeating incumbent Assemblymember Michael DenDekker. González-Rojas, who was endorsed by Tiffany Cabán but interestingly enough not AOC, is now the fourth Latina to be elected in Queens, following the elections of AOC, Jessica Ramos, and Catalina Cruz two years ago.

Two things are important about these successes: First, that we are seeing the rise of female representation among Latino political representatives. Latinas have rightly felt emboldened by the lack of progress that was evident in our communities and have responded by elbowing their way to the table, knowing that they have something to offer and contribute to Latino communities. And the communities are responding by electing them.

Currently, there are 31 Latino elected officials in the city, including the addition of González-Rojas. Women now represent 42% of all Latino elected officials in the city—from Congress to the City Council. (Here, I am not including the numerous women that hold party positions.) While there is much more to do to make that figure more representative of the Latina presence within the electorate and society at large, the trend is encouraging.

With the re-election of the women mentioned above, and the election of González-Rojas, the 2020 primary election cycle may come to be known as the year of the Latina. It's about time! I am certain that the late Olga Mendez, the first Latina in the country to be elected to the state Legislature (representing East Harlem for many years) is smiling from above.

Additionally, the addition of González-Rojas to Queens' representation also marks a shift in the center of Latino voter participation and presence. Whereas formerly the Bronx was almost exclusively where Latino elected officials resided, we are now seeing the results of what has been a steady increase in the Latino population in Queens. As we've seen with AOC, Ramos, Cruz, and now González-Rojas, more Latino candidates are being elected in the borough of Queens. The Archie Bunker days seem to be over. A new era is being ushered in.

In the future, I will take a deeper dive into the significance of the Latino vote in this primary cycle. For now, as results continue to trickle in and as we await the Board of Elections' counting of absentee ballots and certification of outcomes, the Latino community should be proud of its seeming awakening.

PART TWO

2021–2025

8

Latinos and the 2021 New York City Mayoral Election

WILL LATINOS FINALLY HELP elect the first Latino mayor in New York City history? With a term-limited Bill de Blasio, and with Latinos a growing political force in Gotham, two Latino candidates on the Democratic side are vying to replace him in Gracie Mansion and Fernando Mateo has just announced his candidacy to gain the Republican nomination.

Brooklyn City Council Member Carlos Menchaca and long-time nonprofit executive Dianne Morales have positioned themselves within the progressive wing of the Democratic Party as they seek the city's top job. Both come to this mayoral race with considerably less name recognition than two previous top-tier Latino candidates that sought the mayoralty, Herman Badillo and Fernando Ferrer.

Badillo, the first Latino to run competitively for mayor, initiated his quest for the seat in 1969, having served as Bronx Borough President for the previous three years. Badillo also gained some notoriety as a commissioner in the John Lindsey mayoral administration.

Ferrer, who also served as Bronx Borough President and as a City Council member before that, sought the mayoralty in 2001 and again in 2005. Badillo never did secure the Democratic nomination (nor the Republican one in 2001). Ferrer did—but subsequently lost to then-Mayor Michael Bloomberg in the 2005 general election.

The context in which Menchaca and Morales find themselves is vastly different from that of Badillo and Ferrer. For one, the Latino base is much more diverse in its ethnic and cultural makeup. For another, the internal dynamics of the Democratic Party seem to be shifting from racial and ethnic identity politics to ideological positioning.

Regarding the diversity found in Latino communities in New York, we see that Puerto Ricans, historically the largest Latino group in New York, are no longer the only ones representing Latinos. Today, New York City has a large number of Dominican, Colombian, Ecuadorian, and Peruvian elected officials. The Bronx, once a hub of Puerto Rican presence, now has the largest Dominican community in the city, and Queens is a hub for Ecuadorians and Colombians. Brooklyn also exemplifies the diversity of the Latino community, including the presence of a significant cluster of Mexican hermanos and hermanas in Sunset Park, for instance, which is part of the district represented by Menchaca, who is Mexican-American. Morales is of Puerto Rican descent.

The diversity among Latinos in New York is worth celebrating. But will this diverse Latino community vote as a bloc and become the power base that it can be? Will New York City elect its first Latino mayor?

Comprising a quarter of the Democratic primary electorate, Latinos are a force to be reckoned with. But by itself the Latino vote is insufficient to elect a candidate, even if the candidate is a Latino. To win, the candidate will need to build coalitions across ideological, geographical, and ethnic differences. The one Latino candidate that was seen as having a viable path from Grand Concourse to Gracie Mansion was Ruben Diaz, Jr. With a sizable campaign warchest and some name recognition as Bronx Borough President, Diaz Jr. would have surely positioned himself among the top-tier candidates on the Democratic side, but he decided not to run.

For the two Democratic Latino contenders this year, forming such a coalition will be difficult, even with the new ranked-choice voting system. Morales and Menchaca remain largely unknown entities at a citywide level. And both candidates, especially Menchaca, lag behind in fundraising and have not received the public matching funds that could give their campaigns new life (Morales says she will hit the requisite threshold at the next filing in March).

Largely because Republicans are vastly outnumbered in New York City, Mateo would have practically no chance of winning the mayoralty, even if he were to win the Republican primary.

Despite challenges, Morales has proven to be a formidable candidate, developing fascinating policy proposals that will appeal to many primary voters. Unfortunately, this may not be enough. But if that's the case, Morales' efforts will nonetheless likely help forge a path for her to run for elected office again in the future.

Based on the current crop of Latino candidates and the current dynamics in the mayoral race, Latinos will likely have to wait longer for one of their own to finally become mayor of Gotham City. But with a sufficiently strong voting electoral presence in June, Latinos can again demonstrate that they are a force to be taken seriously and a growing base upon which to win a mayoral race.

9

Latinos and the 2021 New York
City Council Elections

IN THE COMING MONTHS, leading up to the all-important June New York City primary elections, I will be writing a series of columns for Gotham Gazette exploring how the Latino vote can impact City Council races across the city. The series—Latino Vote '21—will also highlight some opportunities that may increase Latino political representation and will at times touch on citywide or boroughwide races.

This series is, I believe, the first of its kind in a publication like Gotham Gazette. Past analytical pieces that have explored the Latino vote and Latino political representation, like those by the late Angelo Falcón, were published primarily in academic journals or for think tank-like entities like Falcon's own National Institute for Latino Policy. I'm grateful for the opportunity to shed light on a pivotal ethnic group that could further shift the dynamics of our city's politics.

The rise in the Latino voting population in New York City has long been explored, including by me at Gotham Gazette.[1] Yet it is worth repeating here that Latinos are now the largest ethnic voting group in the city among all active registered voters, and among Democratic voters, they

---

1. Valentin, "2020 Primaries."

represent the second largest ethnic voting group in the city, ahead of white voters and just 80,000 behind African-Americans.

The one difference between Latinos and these two other largest racial groups is that Latinos have so far not been avid voters. But they could be. If they were, they could affect the course of New York City electoral politics quite significantly. And in fact, we have seen glimpses of hope for Latinos in the last two primary election cycles. According to voter data company L2, the 2018 and 2020 primary elections in New York each drew over 100,000 Latinos to the polls.

If these Latino voting patterns continue, Latinos could finally represent a quarter of the entire Democratic electorate in June. In turn this will determine who occupies the West Wing of City Hall, and the East Wing, where City Council Members do their business.

In the weeks to come, this series will take a borough-by-borough approach. It will look at specific City Council races in Latino-majority districts, and districts with a sizable enough number of Latino voters to affect the outcome of such races. The articles will be filled with demographic analysis, and information on candidates and stakeholders in the districts. That analysis and information will, I hope, help readers make informed voting decisions, and draw attention to important matters that may affect your life and those of your neighbors.

The implications of the 2021 New York City elections—which will for the first time include ranked-choice voting in party primaries and special elections—could have pivotal implications for our future as Latinos in the city. Anyone running for city office will need to listen to increasingly vocal and informed Latinos if they wish to pass by the store-front taquerias, cuchifritos, and barberias of our streets on their way to City Hall.

10

Latinos and the 2021 City Council Elections in the Bronx

I MENTIONED IN MY previous column[1] introducing this series on the Latino vote in the 2021 New York City elections that the growing Latino presence in New York has meant a slow but steady increase in Latino voting participation. This increase may possibly lead to greater Latino representation across the city. This city election cycle—with all of city government on the ballot in June primaries and a fall general election—can prove this theory right or wrong.

We begin our exploration in the Bronx, the borough Latinos call "El Condado de la Salsa" (the borough of Salsa music), with five City Council districts that are contested and have large Latino populations—Council districts 11, 13, 14, 15, and 18.

I am deliberately omitting district 16, which I briefly highlight here because interestingly enough the district is majority Latino. However, even there, Latino voting participation lags behind other ethnic groups, with African-Americans and a growing African population being the next largest groups. The district has been represented by African-Americans for decades, the most recent being Vanessa Gibson, who is now running for Bronx borough president. Helen Foster represented the district before

---

1. Valentin, "Latinos and the 2021 New York City Council Elections."

Gibson, and replaced her father, Wendell Foster. While Latinos make up the largest group in the district, no Latino candidates are on the ballot for the June primary this year.

Our look into the Council districts begins in the northwestern part of the Bronx, the 11th district. Eric Dinowitz, son of Assemblymember Jeffrey Dinowitz, recently won a special election, besting a number of candidates, one of whom was a Latina, Mino Lora, who is running again in the June primary. The 11th Council district demographically points to a trend that is happening in other parts of the city—Latinos have outpaced other ethnic groups in voting population numbers. Interestingly, Latinos are now the largest ethnic group in this district that has been historically represented by non-Latinos.

In addition to Lora, who has received the endorsement of a number of progressive groups and leaders, Marcos Sierra, a current Democratic District leader, is the other Latino in the race. Having two Latinos on the ballot does not bode well for either of them since it presents the likelihood of a divided Latino vote.

Further east, the 13th Council district is currently represented by Mark Gjonaj, who is not running for re-election. It is likely that Latinos will gain representation with this open seat, especially since Marjorie Velazquez, a top candidate for the position, has garnered much support and is the only candidate in this race that has received public matching money (she narrowly lost to Gjonaj four years ago). A Velazquez win will not only increase Latino representation at the Council but also increase female representation in that august legislative body that has seen a significant gender imbalance.

Further west lies the 14th Council district. I believe this open seat, currently represented by term-limited Bronx borough president candidate Fernando Cabrera, will be the most contested seat in the Bronx. There are six candidates on the ballot and five of the six have already received over $100,000 in public matching money. Several, like Haile Rivera, Yudelka Tapia, and Adolfo Abreu have had long-standing relationships and community work in the district. Fernando Aquino, also contending for the post, was a communications director for former Attorney General Eric Schneiderman, and Pierina Sanchez has garnered the support of numerous elected officials and labor unions. This race is one to watch.

Right next door to the 14th is the 15th Council district. Oswald Feliz recently won the special election there to replace Ritchie Torres, who won his election to Congress last June. Some of the other candidates that ran in that election will vie for the post again in June, including Ischia Bravo, who garnered labor support in her bid for the seat. Feliz, whose victory surprised many observers, had the support of Congressional Rep. Adriano Espaillat.

Feliz's victory in the 15th Council district is the first for a Dominican. The seat has been represented by Puerto Ricans for decades. This victory marks a shift that has long been observed because of the steady increase of Dominicans in New York. It is clear that Dominican voters have now become a powerhouse in the Bronx. Though according to modeled data by the likes of prominent voter data companies L2 and Catalist, Puerto Ricans still outnumber Dominicans in the voting population, Dominicans are quickly inching their way to the top. Feliz's victory points to this reality.

The last Council district we are looking at in the Bronx is the 18th. After serving a term in the Council and losing to Ritchie Torres in last year's congressional race, the Rev. Ruben Diaz Sr. has decided not to seek re-election. Several candidates are vying for the seat, including some returning contestants like Michael Beltzer and Amanda Farias. There's also William Rivera, the district manager of Community Board 9, who recently received the endorsement of outgoing Bronx Borough President, Ruben Diaz Jr. Others who are on the ballot and have received public funding include Mohammed Mujumder, who received the maximum.

The two front-runners seem to be Farias and Rivera. Farias has earned the support of many labor and activist organizations and elected officials across the city, and has received the maximum in public funds. Rivera, who has also received the maximum and now Diaz, Jr.'s endorsement, will be a top contender and would need to use every penny possible to offset the organizing efforts of labor and others on behalf of Farias. A Farias victory would see the return of Latina representation at the Council in this district some years after the district was represented by Annabel Palma.

All in all, the quality of Latino candidates in the Bronx—the city's most-Latino borough—is impressive, especially since there appears to be an increase in political activity among young Latinos, evident by the number of hotly-contested races featuring young Latino candidates.

My next column will look at another hotly contested race in the Bronx, this one the big enchilada—the Borough President's race.

11

The Latino Vote and the 2021 Bronx Borough President Race

TERM LIMITS MEAN A slew of hotly-contested races every eight years in New York City. This year, not only is the mayor's race in this category, but the race to succeed outgoing Bronx Borough President Ruben Diaz, Jr. is too, yet it is one that is unfortunately attracting little attention.

The Bronx borough president race has five candidates on the ballot: Fernando Cabrera, Nathalia Fernandez, Vanessa Gibson, Sammy Ravelo, and Luis Sepulveda. Four of these five candidates are currently in elected office, come to the race with some name recognition in their respective districts, and are funded adequately with public matching money.

Historically, the Bronx Borough President position has been significant for Latinos. As the only Latino-majority borough in the City of New York, the Bronx has elected four Latinos to represent its borough in the last 50 years. The first Latino elected to the position was the iconic Herman Badillo, who won the position in 1965. Badillo's victory was a pivotal moment in New York City Latino political history, and came at a time at which the Latino population in the borough (mostly Puerto Rican) was growing. This growth eventually led to an increase in Latino political representation; one that, at least in the Bronx, was paved by the likes of Badillo.

Badillo went on to run for mayor a number of times, but fell short of making history by being the first Latino to occupy Gracie Mansion. Twenty years later, Fernando Ferrer became the second Latino to occupy the seat of Bronx borough president. During his 14 years of service, the "Bronx is burning" image of the borough began to dissipate. New development and new businesses replaced abandoned buildings, and with them came more jobs. Ferrer then tried to take his vision citywide, running for mayor in 2001 and 2005. He won the Democratic primary in 2005 but lost to Michael Bloomberg in the general election. Since then, Latinos have not had another prominent and recognized Latino candidate for mayor.

Adolfo Carrion succeeded Ferrer and like him made a bid for Gracie Mansion, but fell well short. In a special election to replace Carrion, who had accepted a position in the Obama White House, Ruben Diaz, Jr. won and has been the borough president since. Diaz, Jr. was at one point a candidate for the mayoralty and was considered in the top tier until he dropped out of the race.

All four of the Latino borough presidents in the Bronx, by virtue of the (largely symbolic) influence of their borough-wide posts, positioned themselves for the mayoralty and have been, until Dianne Morales' current candidacy, the only credible and viable Latino candidates for the mayoralty.

Having several viable Latino candidates on the ballot, all from different sections of the Bronx, may splinter the Latino vote, paving the way for a possible victory by Vanessa Gibson and the first non-Latino Bronx borough president in 35 years. The current voter rolls give us an indication that this may be a distinct possibility. Among the entire Democratic electorate, Latinos make up the largest share among all ethnic categories in the Bronx, with 285,586 voters. Black voters are second with 191,944.

My theory has some quantifiable backing in the poll[1] commissioned by StudentsFirstNY and undertaken by the reputable Benenson Strategy Group. The poll shows Gibson with a lead and the Latino candidates receiving between 9% and 12% of the vote-share among those polled.

Of the four Latinos in this year's borough president race, City Council Member Fernando Cabrera has raised the most money and has received more public matching money than any other candidate. While he comes into the race with significant legislative experience, his conservative social values have been a cause of concern for many in the borough.

Nathalia Fernandez is the only Latina in the race and placed second in the aforementioned April poll. She has the least amount of money left in her coffers, so she may run into some difficulty getting her message across

---

1. Students First NY, "New York City Democratic Primary Poll."

to a borough-wide electorate. Sepulveda and Ravelo round out the rest of the field.

Though this is an expansive, borough-wide race, media exposure and voter attention will largely be focused on the mayoral race. These next few weeks are therefore a critical time for the candidates to get their names and message before the Bronx electorate.

Will Latinos splinter their votes? If so, will the Bronx, the only Latino-majority borough in the city, elect its first non-Latino borough president in 35 years? We'll know soon.

12

Latinos and the 2021 City Council Elections in Queens

THE LATINO POPULATION IN Queens has exploded over the last two decades, and it is prompting a coming of age in Latino political representation in the borough. If current trends continue, Queens may become another center of Latino political power in the City of New York, alongside the Bronx.

The rise of Latino political representation in Queens began in 2000 when Hiram Monserrate became the first Latino elected to a position in the borough, beating an incumbent for a Democratic district leader position. One year later, he became the first Latino from Queens to be elected to the City Council. While acknowledging his eventual conviction, one cannot ignore Monserrate, for in many ways he paved the way for other Latinos to win and hold local office.

Many of them, including former City Council Member Julissa Ferreras and current State Senator Jessica Ramos, were once members of his staff. Others, like the late Jose Peralta, were not only allies of Monserrate but Monserrate lent them his once effective organization for their electoral pursuits and eventual victories. To be clear, both Ferreras and Ramos disavowed Monserrate after his conviction. Peralta ran against Monserrate after his scandals and beat him in a special election for the State Senate seat that had once belonged to him.

As Latinos have increased in number in the overall and voting populations, the number of Latino elected officials has likewise increased. In addition to the names already mentioned, Francisco Moya (who is up for re-election and is facing a formidable challenge from Ingrid Gomez), Catalina Cruz, Jessica Gonzalez-Rojas, and of course Alexandria Ocasio-Cortez have all won legislative seats representing Queens. Other Latinos have won positions as Democratic district leaders in the borough.

The ramifications of this growth among Latinos will again be felt in this year's elections—all of city government is on the ballot in this month's primaries and the fall general election, with many competitive City Council races in Queens and across the five boroughs, as well as the races for mayor, comptroller, public advocate, and borough presidencies.

It is quite possible that the number of Latino elected officials in Queens will increase by as much as five (though I anticipate a gain of three), as the demographic changes in some City Council districts have tilted heavily from majority white to majority Latino.

In the 22nd Council District, based in Astoria, Tiffany Caban is a favorite for the seat left vacant by Council Member Costa Constantinides, who was term-limited but resigned recently due to family reasons and another job opportunity. Interestingly, this district is not majority Latino, though Latinos make up a quarter of the Democratic electorate, according to L2 voter data. Caban's strength lies in the fact that she comes to the race off an incredible run for district attorney, where she barely lost to Melinda Katz in a recount, and thus has considerable name recognition and other advantages. Furthermore, Caban is a darling of the progressive left, many of whom reside in this district. Together, this makes her a serious contender for the seat and therefore increases the possibility of another Latina being elected in the borough of Queens.

Further west, we come to the 25th Council District, the seat currently held by outgoing Council Member Danny Dromm, who is term-limited. This district, covering Jackson Heights and Elmhurst, has seen one of the largest increases in the Latino population in the entire borough, making it now a majority-Latino district. Of the Democratic electorate, an estimated 41% is Latino. The next closest group is South Asians at 20% of the Democratic electorate. Four of the eight candidates running in the all-important Democratic primary are Latinos: Liliana Melo, Manuel Perez, Alfonso Quiroz, and William Salgado. Of the four, Melo and Quiroz have received over $140,000 in public matching money, significantly boosting their campaigns. This race is one to watch.

Another Council district with a rapidly increasing Latino community is Queens' 26th, covering parts or all of Sunnyside, Woodside, Long Island City, Astoria, and Dutch Kills. Its current occupant, Jimmy Van Bremer, is term-limited and thus cannot seek re-election to the Council. White voters only outnumber Latinos by an estimated 1,125 Democratic voters. Considering the trend of continued growth among Latinos, it is likely that in the next few years this district will also become majority-Latino. Two of the 15 candidates are Latinos: Lorenzo Brea and Glennis Gomez. Both have received public matching money and are competitive, creating another opportunity to increase Latino representation in the borough.

The 30th Council District is the fourth Queens district presenting Latinos an opportunity to increase representation this year. Covering the neighborhoods of Glendale, Maspeth, Middle Village, Ridgewood, Woodhaven, and Woodside, this district is now majority-Latino. Latinos have a slight edge in the Democratic primary (by just an estimated 61 voters) over white voters in what has been a white-ethnic enclave for many decades. Juan Ardila is taking on incumbent Council Member Robert Holden, who is up for re-election after he lost the Democratic primary in a 2017 bid to unseat Elizabeth Crowley, then defeated her in the general election running on the Republican and other ballot lines.

Ardila has proven to be a solid fundraiser, and like Holden, he has received the maximum in public matching money. Endorsed by Donovan Richards (the current borough president), State Senator Ramos, the Working Families Party, and many progressive groups, elected officials, and labor unions, Ardila has a good chance of defeating one of the few incumbents in this election cycle, at least in the primary.

The last Queens Council district I am looking at in terms of Latino representation is the 32nd. Eric Ulrich, one of the few Republicans in the Council, is the current occupant and is term-limited from running again. Latinos are now the majority of the Democratic electorate, though not a majority of the overall vote. Bella Matias is the only Latina on the ballot and has received over $52,000 in public matching money. If she is able to organize and turn out enough Latino votes in a crowded race, she may surprise some observers, though whoever wins will still have to defeat the Republican nominee in the general election in a district that has more Democrats than Republicans but has elected Ulrich several times.

On primary day and as the votes are counted over the following weeks, my eyes will be focused on Queens. With its sizable and growing Latino presence, Queens may well send even more Latinos to City Hall.

13

A Big Boost for Eric Adams in the Democratic Primary for Mayor

THE DEMOCRATIC MAYORAL PRIMARY is finally over. Over too is the ranked-choice vote counting process. We know enough for a preliminary analysis of how many Latinos voted and how, though those numbers will need to be fine-tuned after results have been certified and voter information updated.

Here is what we know right now: In a crowded field, Eric Adams earned the greatest chunk of the Latino vote, especially in the Bronx, the only Latino-majority borough in the City of New York. It appears that Adams won over 50% of the first-choice votes in the election districts with the highest number of Latino voters. That's an impressive feat considering that there were 13 candidates vying for the Democratic nomination, including one Latina (Dianne Morales) and another candidate with a Latino surname (Kathryn Garcia). Though the obvious second choice for many Latinos might have been Morales or Garcia, in fact, election night results show they voted overwhelmingly for Maya Wiley (again, in terms of first-rank votes, we will eventually seek how all the ranked ballots turned out).

Adams' performance among Latinos in other boroughs was not as decisive as in the Bronx, though he garnered at least a third of the first-rank votes in election districts with high Latino concentrations and won most of them. Take the 72nd Assembly District in Washington Heights: there, Adams earned almost 33% of first-place votes, the most of any candidate.

Wiley received a quarter of the first-place vote in this overwhelmingly Latino district. Of course, this is the home district of Congressional Rep. Adriano Espaillat, who eventually endorsed Adams, and City Council Member Ydanis Rodriguez, who was a strong supporter from early in the campaign.

This same Adams-Wiley dynamic is evident in majority Latino election districts in Brooklyn (Cypress Hills, and parts of Bushwick, East New York, and Williamsburg), Manhattan (East Harlem, the Lower East Side, and Washington Heights), and Queens (Corona, East Elmhurst, Jackson Heights).

Why was Adams' performance among Latinos decisive in the Bronx and not as impressive in the other boroughs? Here are my hunches.

On one hand, Adams earned critical endorsements in the condado de la Salsa. Borough President Ruben Diaz Jr., Rep. Espaillat (whose district covers Upper Manhattan and much of the West Bronx), Assemblymember José Rivera, City Council Member Rafael Salamanca, and former Borough President Fernando Ferrer all endorsed Adams. (Congressional Rep. Ritchie Torres announced Adams as his second pick after Andrew Yang.)

Were the Diaz Jr. and Espaillat endorsements a key moment for Latino voter preference in the Bronx—besides Adams' own campaign operations and the independent expenditure support there, of course? And what was the full impact of Espaillat's nod? Remember that in the past he has not only given his name to candidates but has also lent them his well-oiled campaign apparatus. The most obvious example of this was Oswald Feliz's victory in the special election to succeed Torres in the City Council.

One must also evaluate the potential significance of Adams' message of public safety. Presumably sensible and just public safety enforcement is a message that resonates with Latinos more than acknowledged. Since much of the violent crime occurs in Black and Brown neighborhoods, increasingly in the Bronx, this is hardly surprising. Adams also spoke clearly to key issues like the struggles for small business owners and the quality of the city's public schools, which are both high on the list for many Latino voters, and pledged to address them.

There are many reasons why Eric Adams earned the biggest chunk of the Latino vote, the largest share coming from the Bronx. Latinos formed an essential part of the coalition Adams needed to move him past the Democratic primary and into the general election in November.

14

The Case for a Latino
Lieutenant Governor

ANDREW CUOMO'S RESIGNATION HAS historical import in potentially numerous ways. When the current Lieutenant Governor, Kathy Hochul, becomes Governor of New York in just under two weeks, she will become the first woman to occupy the executive chamber in Albany. History will also be made if Hochul decides to appoint a Latino as her Lieutenant Governor. I suggest that is exactly what she should do. Why?

First, Latinos now make up the largest ethnic voting bloc in the entire state. Yet there is no Latino representation within leadership at the state executive and legislative levels. Hochul is a white woman from the Buffalo area. The current Senate Majority Leader is Andrea Stewart-Cousins, an African-American woman from Westchester. The Speaker of the Assembly is Carl Heastie, an African-American man from the Bronx. Our current State Attorney General is Letitia James, an African-American woman from Brooklyn, and State Comptroller is Thomas DiNapoli, a white man from Long Island.

Even among the leaders of the respective county political organizations in New York City, there is no longer any Latino representation. And this includes the Bronx, which is the only Latino-majority borough in the city. Four of the five Democratic organizations in the city are represented by African-Americans. Furthermore, Brooklyn Borough President Eric

Adams, also African-American, is likely to be our next Mayor. The current and likely continuing Public Advocate, Jumaane Williams, is also African-American and of Brooklyn. The likely next City Comptroller, another Brooklynite, is Brad Lander, a white man.

Truly, the above list shows a major feat for our African-American sisters and brothers who have fought so hard for proper and due representation at all levels of government and political party organizations. Yet, based on sheer numbers and proven ability, it would seem that Latinos should also be recognized with high-level appointments and elections.

Second, there are several highly-qualified Latino elected officials and non-elected individuals who could serve the next Governor and the people of New York well. Among the Latinos that have great public policy chops, are thoughtful, articulate, and charismatic, and could potentially inhabit this position well are the following:

RUBEN DIAZ, JR.

Diaz, Jr. is term-limited out of his position as Bronx Borough President and decided not to run for mayor. He has extensive Albany experience, having served as an Assemblymember for over a decade. Diaz, Jr. has served as borough president for the last 12 years and during this time he has helped oversee and usher in advancements for Bronxites and growth in his beloved borough. He is generally well-liked and well-respected. I would not be surprised if other Latinos inside and outside government lobby hard for his selection.

FERNANDO FERRER

One cannot discount Fernando Ferrer as a potential consideration. He was Bronx Borough President for 14 years, and most recently served as acting chair of the MTA. There is no doubt that Ferrer is a widely respected figure with vast experience and would serve the new governor well.

LATINAS IN THE MIX?

There are a number of Latinas that deserve Hochul's attention too. Some are already in elected office, and others no longer in office could also be formidable candidates for the position of Lieutenant Governor. Some that could be in the mix are the former Speaker of the City Council, Melissa Mark-Viverito, and former Council Member Margarita Lopez, among others.

There are other Latino leaders, like State Senators Jessica Ramos and Gustavo Rivera, who could be considered by Hochul but do not appear to match her politics as well as other possible appointees. While unlikely, she could look to appoint one of them as a way to reach out to not only Latinos but the left wing of the Democratic Party.

Among the appointed Latino officials who could be under consideration: New York Secretary of State Rossana Rosado.

WHAT OF THE CONGRESSIONAL REPRESENTATIVES?

New York City currently has four Democratic Latino congressional representatives: Adriano Espaillat, Alexandria Ocasio-Cortez, Ritchie Torres, and Nydia Velazquez. With a House majority, and these representatives playing important roles in Congress, I don't expect any of them to accept a position with virtually no power, other than being a heartbeat away from the executive chamber . . . or a resignation away from being Governor. There is also the uncertainty of the future given Hochul and her Lieutenant Governor will have to run for a full term next year.

The makings are there for Latinos to have a representative at the statewide level. Will Hochul herself quickly make history again with her first major appointment? Let's hope so.

15

Latino Vote '21

A Closer Look at the 2021 Democratic Primary

FOUR YEARS AGO I participated in a forum on the theme of Latino politics and voting participation in New York hosted by the Rev. Ray Rivera of the Latino Pastoral Action Center in the Bronx. The forum was based largely on two columns I had recently written here at Gotham Gazette—and "The Future of Latino Politics in New York City."[1]

I was the new kid on the block, the "new" Latino political analyst thrust on this panel with two legendary figures: the late Angelo Falcon, the first Puerto Rican political analyst to grace our city, and Juan Cartagena, another pivotal leader and the past head of the renowned LatinoJustice.

I came armed with the most up-to-date political data and the analytical tools gained from years of employing political targeting methods. I came gleeful about the future of Latino politics in New York: Latinos could no longer be taken for granted or ignored. The moment we had predicted decades earlier, of increased Latino electoral participation and increased power, was right around the corner. The sleeping giant had finally awakened.

Falcon, a seasoned observer who had studied Latino voting patterns and trends since I was in elementary school, gently and diplomatically put me in my place. "I am not as optimistic about the future of Latino politics as my colleague Eli," he said. Falcon was right.

---

1. Valentin, "Future of Latino Politics in New York City."

Looking back at this most recent primary in New York City, the consequential June 2021 elections, armed with more data and perspective, it's true that: The primary attracted the second highest Latino voter turnout rate in any primary in New York City.

This was the largest overall Latino voter turnout in a municipal election. Latinos were a pivotal voting bloc for Eric Adams' primary victory, with, for example, the Brooklyn borough president garnering close to 50% of the vote in the highest Latino election districts in the Bronx despite the very crowded and competitive field of candidates.

But that's where the good ends and Falcon's past skepticism comes in. My projection that Latinos would make up close to a quarter of the Democratic primary electorate fell well short. True, Latinos compose a quarter of all registered Democratic voters (a total of 3,444,859 Democrats) in New York City, but Latinos were only 15% of the roughly 935,294 Democratic voters in that June primary.

In the June 2020 and September 2018 primaries, Latinos made up a little over 20% of the Democratic electorate. These were potential signs of an awakened Latino electorate. But my hopes for this potential came crashing down this year.

More troubling is the fact that only 17% of the 864,511 registered Democratic Latino voters in New York City went to the polls this past June. The Bronx has the highest number of Latino Democratic voters with 283,573 but had the lowest turnout rate, 14%, among Latinos in all the boroughs.

Meanwhile, 20% of Manhattan Latinos went to the polls, the highest among Latinos in all boroughs, and 17% of Brooklyn, Queens, and Staten Island Latinos went to the polls.

Though this incoming City Council class will have the highest number of Latino representatives at 14 of the 51-seat legislative body, Latinos could have potentially won at least two more seats (in districts 25 and 32) had more Latinos voted. Could a higher turnout among Latinos also have kept a Latino helming Borough Hall in the Bronx, the only borough in the city that is majority Latino? Perhaps.

The biggest hindrance for Latino political representation and power in New York City are Latinos themselves.

What can Latino political and community leaders do about this? Let's begin by taking opportunities like the annual November SOMOS conference in Puerto Rico to strategize how to mobilize Latino voters across the city.

16

A Latino Assessment of Bill de Blasio's Mayoralty

"De parte de Chirlane, Chiara, Dante y yo, les extiendo las gracias a ustedes, mis hermanas y hermanos niuyorquinos, por acompañarnos en este dia tan especial."

—Mayor Bill de Blasio, Inaugural Address, January 1, 2014

After the usual pleasantries that are part and parcel of such events, Bill de Blasio buoyed our spirits with these words on January 1st, 2014, during his inaugural mayoral address. Surely, they were a clear and welcome indication that he would connect with those often forgotten in New York, in this case Latinos, an ethnic group that had become the new powerhouse in Gotham City. Was this the dawning of a new—and progressive—era in Gotham, one in which Latinos would no longer be excluded? Surely so! After all, De Blasio was promising to do away with conditions that had made a tale of two cities the reality in New York, a tale of previous mayoral administrations' failed policies that had dashed the hopes and dreams of Latinos. But apparently promises are made to be broken.

Eight years after his mayoralty, it's clear that de Blasio's promise to Latinos went unfulfilled during his administration of the city. Truth be told, there were early indications that de Blasio would not take Latinos seriously.

Just two weeks before de Blasio took office as mayor, the late Angel Falcon called to task the then mayor-elect for not appointing enough Latinos to prominent positions in the new administration.[1] Almost one year later, Falcon continued his push for fair Latino representation, noting that though Latinos made up 29 percent of the city's population, they composed only 12 percent of all appointments of the still young de Blasio mayoral administration. There was still time for de Blasio to take Latinos seriously. But he chose not to. Falcon's concern for equity among mayoral appointees compelled him to form *Latinos for Fair Representation* alongside other Latino leaders like Javier Nieves. Three years later, as de Blasio prepared himself to cruise to re-election, Latino underrepresentation in the halls of city government continued unabated.[2]

Beyond Latino representation in government, de Blasio's policy failures have been evident in some of the most important issues facing New York City Latinos. The economic conditions of Latinos in the city, for instance, did not improve during de Blasio's tenure. His quest to combat income inequality and end the "tale of two cities" failed. By de Blasio's second term, Latinos were still the poorest ethnic group citywide, with more than half of their children living below the poverty line.

Latino families also did not benefit from de Blasio's ambitious affordable housing plan, one which sought to create or preserve 200,000 affordable housing units. According to a Princeton University study[3], many Latino families spend half of their income on housing costs, a clear indication that de Blasio's housing plan has had no positive impact for Latinos. Moreover, Latinos have also faced astronomical rates of racial discrimination from landlords. The study states, "Compared to whites, [Latinos] are 28 percent less likely to have a landlord return their calls and 49 percent less likely to receive an offer at all."

On perhaps de Blasio's signature accomplishment, universal pre-K, vast disparities in classroom quality exists between white and Latino children, according to a Brown University report.[4]

The jury is still out on how de Blasio handled the COVID-19 pandemic and its aftermath, but let's not forget that it hit Latino neighborhoods the

1. Sora, "Latino Group Slams de Blasio."
2. Borges, "Latinos Get the Shaft Again."
3. Kelly, "Hispanics Face Racial Discrimination."
4. Latham et al., "Racial Disparities in Pre-K Quality."

hardest. A UCLA study[5] has shown that Latinos have been 1.4 times more likely than Whites to be infected with the virus and twice as likely to be hospitalized and to die from it. To add insult to injury, vaccination rates among Latinos have been significantly lower than Whites, calling into question the handling of this disparity by the current mayoral administration.

All in all, as we weigh the impact on Latinos of key issues in New York City, it's clear that de Blasio failed to achieve his stated goals as mayor, even when considering his major policy initiatives. With the Latino population constituting almost a third of the city's population, the lack of Latino representation in city government is frankly inexcusable. History will not look kindly on de Blasio's mayoralty . . . and with good reason.

5. Ong et al., "COVID-19 Death and Vaccination Rates for Latinos in New York City."

17

Will Latinos Lose the First Assembly Seat They Won 84 Years Ago?

The Looming Battle in East Harlem

How might Assemblymember Robert Rodriguez's resignation lead to Puerto Ricans losing the seat for which they have fought so long? Let me explain.

Last week, as a who's who of New York elected officials descended on the island of Puerto Rico, Governor Kathy Hochul was preparing her continued push to revamp state government, attempting along the way the diversification of the Empire State's governmental representatives.

On Thursday, 1,600 miles away from New York and under the hot Caribbean sun in Borinquen, Hochul announced the appointment of Assemblymember Rodriguez of East Harlem to the position of Secretary of State. Rodriguez becomes the fifth consecutive Latino to be appointed to the position.

Rodriguez's appointment will set off a royal rumble, with numerous individuals already declaring their intentions to succeed him in the Assembly. Rodriguez's seat is one that has significant historical importance for Latino politics in New York.

It was in 1937 that the first Latino to win elected office in New York, the Puerto Rican Oscar Garcia Rivera, occupied this very seat in East Harlem. (East Harlem would come to be known as a place of firsts for Latino political representation. Tony Mendez would become the first Latino

Democratic District Leader in 1957. And his daughter-in-law, Olga Mendez, would become the first Puerto Rican woman in the nation to win a seat in a state legislature.)

By the time Garcia Rivera was elected to the State Assembly, East Harlem had become the hub for new Puerto Rican migrants arriving in New York. To be sure, East Harlem was not the initial destination for the first major wave of Puerto Rican migrants. That distinction belonged to Brooklyn, with many Puerto Ricans arriving in Williamsburg and the Brooklyn Navy Yard as a result of the neighborhoods' proximity to the New York City waterways. Puerto Ricans eventually made East Harlem their hub and in time it was first there that Latinos' base of political operations and eventual electoral successes took place. The sheer number of Puerto Ricans that filled the streets of East Harlem led to its unofficial name change to "El Barrio," as it continues to be known today.

Even before the election of Garcia Rivera, Puerto Ricans had become a sought-after voting bloc in East Harlem. Fiorello La Guardia, before his election to the mayoralty, represented East Harlem in Congress. His foresight and close observation of the demographic changes engulfing his neighborhood led La Guardia to foresee the powerful bloc Puerto Ricans would eventually become. His protégé and successor, Vito Marcantonio, also recognized the importance of the Puerto Rican presence and heavily courted their vote and support. Marcantonio became Boricuas' darling for ensuring that proper constituent services (including hiring Puerto Rican, Spanish-speaking staff) be made available to the newcomers. He also championed Puerto Rican independence as East Harlem's congressman.

By 1937, Puerto Ricans had become a powerful force in East Harlem, not only propelling Marcantonio to victory but electing one of their own—Garcia Rivera. The continued rise in the Puerto Rican population led other racial groups to fear they would lose political power. As a result of these other groups banding together, Garcia Rivera lost his position some years later.

Through the decades, gerrymandered districts largely prevented Puerto Ricans in East Harlem from winning significant elected offices. But then in 1962 (over twenty years after Garcia Rivera), the Puerto Rican Carlos Rios won the East Harlem Assembly seat, only to be outdone by reapportionment a few years later. It wasn't until Angelo Del Toro won this seat in 1974 that Puerto Ricans cemented their hold on it and in East Harlem politics more broadly for decades to come.

Del Toro proved to be a canny and successful Assemblyman, holding on to his seat for 20 years until his untimely death in 1994. In that time, he was appointed chair of the social services committee and then the education committee in the State Assembly. Del Toro was perhaps the first Latino to be appointed to prestigious chairmanships in the state legislature.

Just two years before Del Toro's death, the ambitious, young attorney Nelson Denis attempted to dethrone the powerful Del Toro machine in East Harlem. Denis, with a young 34-year-old Mike Nieves as the consultant guiding the campaign, took on Del Toro and almost beat the 20-year incumbent in the 1994 primary. Del Toro's death a year later spurred a special election, and Denis having been bounced off the ballot opened the path for another young East Harlem leader to win the seat. Francisco Diaz, Jr., who at the time served on the local community board, served for one year, until Denis defeated him in the 1996 Democratic primary.

Adam Clayton Powell, after having served in the City Council for some years, took on the now incumbent Nelson Denis four years later and went on to defeat him handily. Powell served as the East Harlem Assemblyman for 10 years. When he decided not to run for re-election in 2010, the path was open for Robert Rodriguez to win the coveted East Harlem seat. Rodriguez, whose father served in the City Council for a number of years, went into the race with name recognition and a record of community service, serving as chair of the local community board before his electoral victory. He has kept his seat for a decade and will leave office with an impressive record of legislative accomplishments.

With Rodriguez's tenure, Puerto Ricans have held on to this Assembly seat for almost 50 consecutive years. So I return to my opening question: Could Rodriguez's upcoming resignation lead to Puerto Ricans losing the seat for which they have fought so long?

Similar to the drastic demographic changes in East Harlem that Puerto Ricans initiated in the 1920s, one that saw a shift from a largely Italian-dominated community to a Puerto Rican one, a significant demographic reality seems to be engulfing East Harlem today. Like other Latino neighborhoods in the city, East Harlem is suffering from years of gentrification, which has caused the unfortunate displacement of many Puerto Rican families. To be sure, gentrification is not the only factor leading to a decrease in the Puerto Rican population in East Harlem, but it is a significant one.

These demographic changes now seem to be having an electoral consequence. Among all registered voters in East Harlem, whites are now just

3,000 shy of reaching the same voting bloc size as African-American voters. There are currently 20,006 registered white voters in El Barrio, almost a 50% increase within the last 15 years. Latinos, mostly Puerto Ricans, come in at 34,232.

Perhaps more significant is the fact that white voters seem to be voting in greater numbers. For instance, the past June primary saw a whopping 1,000-vote increase from the previous primary in 2020 among white voters, with whites coming in just 300 votes shy of the total Latino vote in East Harlem. Truth be told, the apparent significance of this increase is as much a matter of low voter turnout among Latinos as it is the number of white voters in East Harlem. Nevertheless, the increase of white voters in East Harlem cannot be discounted when we consider the potential dynamics that may be at play in with Rodriguez out of the picture.

The Black vote in East Harlem has historically been a significant one. And Blacks continue to play an important part in East Harlem elections. The significant presence of Blacks in East Harlem has always had the potential of pitting one group against the other. Fortunately, Blacks and Latinos in East Harlem have, for the most part, managed to work together for decades, as can be seen by the alliances made through the leadership of officials like Charles Rangel, Keith Wright, Bill Perkins, and others. More recently, newer Black leaders in East Harlem, like local leader Nina Saxon, have intentionally built alliances between these communities.

Nevertheless, because of their sizable presence in East Harlem, Blacks can also play a role in Puerto Ricans losing this Assembly seat. Several African-Americans have already expressed interest in vying for the soon-to-be vacated seat.

Much is at stake for Puerto Ricans in East Harlem. Will more than a half century of Latino representational struggle soon come to a head in East Harlem? We shall know before long.

18

Redistricting and Latinos in New York

THE NEW YORK STATE Legislature has passed, and Governor Hochul has signed, new district maps for the House of Representatives, the State Assembly, and the State Senate. What do these new lines mean for Latino representation? While space limitations prohibit me from providing an exhaustive analysis, several new district lines are worth noting. Let us begin with Congress.

Of all New York City's four congressional districts represented by Latinos, Congressional Rep. Nydia Velázquez's district has undergone the most deviation from its previous contours. Rep. Velázquez was the first Puerto Rican Latina to be elected to Congress. It appears that her district—New York's 7th Congressional District, covering parts of Brooklyn, Manhattan, and Queens, and with a Latino plurality—has borne the brunt of congressional district changes in the city, a result of deliberate maneuvering in order to make the 11th Congressional District more suitable for a Democratic retaking.

The 11th is currently represented by Rep. Nicole Malliotakis, a Republican and half-Cuban Congress member. NY-11 is the only congressional district in New York City currently represented by a Republican.

Several neighborhoods in NY-7, including Sunset Park and Red Hook, with their sizable Latino presences, have been drawn out of Velázquez's district and into Malliotakis'. Rep. Velázquez has represented Sunset Park since her election to Congress in 1992 and the neighborhood was included in that district at a time when an additional Latino-majority district was sought. Current opponents of the dismantling of parts of Velázquez's district point to the potential of voting dilution, since Latinos in Sunset Park and other neighborhoods will now become part of a non-Latino majority district.

Despite all the changes, particularly the possibility of voting dilution, the Latino presence in the new Velázquez district among the voting population has not shifted much, increasing by 4,000 Latino voters from the current lines. The increase is a result of the new 7th district taking in other parts of Queens that Velázquez had not previously represented, namely portions of Ozone Park.

The Latino voting population in the new NY-13, represented by Rep. Adriano Espaillat, has not shifted much, and Rep. Alexandria Ocasio-Cortez's Latino constituency in her district, NY-14, remains largely unchanged. Interestingly enough, Rep. Ritchie Torres, who represents a Latino-majority district whose Latino representation goes back to Herman Badillo, has lost 11,000 Latino voters (mostly in University Heights), while gaining an additional 18,000 white voters, largely a result of the district's move north to include Riverdale.

In relation to Latino politics and representation, perhaps the more drastic changes to district lines can be found in the Senate and Assembly districts. Of New York City's 95 state legislative districts, there are currently five Latinos in the 63-seat State Senate and 11 in the 150-seat Assembly.

Starting in Manhattan, we can begin our exploration of changes in the historic Latino neighborhood of East Harlem. If there ever were a prime example of how communities can be splintered electorally, East Harlem is the one. East Harlem, a geographically compact location that is majority-Latino with a sizable African-American population, will soon be represented by three state senators instead of the current two. Yes, three senators for one community.

Under the new lines, East Harlem will be represented in the State Senate by Senators Cordell Cleare, Michael Gianaris, and Jose Serrano, assuming they all win reelection this year. The East Harlem State Senate seat has had historic importance since Olga Mendez won the seat in 1978, becoming the first Puerto Rican Latina elected to a state legislature in the country.

In Queens, a new State Senate district has been created, what will be the 17th District, part of how the new maps reflect population shifts favoring New York City and a correction to previously gerrymandered districts to favor Republicans outside the city.

Observers note that the carving out of this seat is a result of the increase in the Latino population in Queens and that in essence this becomes a new "Latino seat."[1] However, the data discloses something entirely different. The Redistricting and You data, excellently compiled by Steven Romalewski at the Center for Urban Research at the CUNY Graduate Center, demonstrates that in overall population, Latinos make up 38% of the population in this new district, just a 6% increase from the current Senate lines. In voting age population, Latinos make up 36% of the population, also a 6% increase.

However, when one considers voter registration numbers, Latinos only outnumber the next highest ethnic group (non-Hispanic whites) by 894. When one takes voting participation into account, the numbers would indicate even more that this district is certainly not a "Latino seat," at least not in the immediate future. Among Democratic voters, non-Hispanic whites in this new district outnumber Latinos by over 5,200 voters, a gap of utmost importance given how often elections in New York City are determined by the Democratic primary.

When it comes to Assembly districts, Queens may also take a hit when it comes to Latino representation. The Corona neighborhood, a mostly Latino community, will now be divided into three Assembly districts.

Most of Corona is currently represented in the Assembly by Catalina Cruz. Interestingly, Corona has produced the first Latino representatives in the borough: Hiram Monserrate (the first Latino elected in the borough) and Julissa Ferreras (the first Latina elected in Queens). Now Corona stands the chance of seeing these historic gains jeopardized, seemingly in order to protect some non-Latino incumbents in other neighborhoods.

The electoral splintering of Latino neighborhoods, in addition to the ongoing gentrification of many of these neighborhoods, does not bode well for Latino representation in the next decade. Is this a result of the lack of Latino representation at the higher levels of state government? It certainly seems that way.

1. Velasquez and Michel, "NYC to Pick Up Two State Senate Seats."

19

Latinos and the 2022 Democratic Primary

THE LATINO VOTE IN New York is, thankfully, becoming the important point of conversation it should be. While there's a ways to go, there is more discussion happening—including a variety of political debates, via the inimitable work of Errol Louis in one of his recent columns[1] as well as a podcast episode[2] he dedicated to the Latino vote with me as his guest, and through this series of pieces and associated podcasts published by Gotham Gazette, among other sources.

I have sought to explicate the intricacies of this burgeoning ethnic group for a number of years, largely through this platform. Despite the increased attention, Latinos seem to still often be an afterthought for many elected and party officials, as was made evident by the recent selection of speakers at last month's state Democratic convention. No Latinos were on the original list of speakers, and it was only after a number of prominent Latinos complained about the snub that party officials scrambled to include three Latinos on the list.

Snubbed or not, disregarded or not, Latinos are and will continue to be an important voting constituency in New York City and State elections.

1. Louis, "New Era for Latino Politics in New York?"
2. Louis, *You Decide with Errol Louis.*

54

Some politicians understand this, like Tom Suozzi, a member of Congress who is now aspiring to defeat Governor Kathy Hochul and others in June's Democratic primary. Suozzi not only named former Bronx Borough President Fernando Ferrer the chair of his campaign; he also named Diana Reyna, former City Council member and deputy Brooklyn Borough President, as his lieutenant governor running-mate.

New York City Public Advocate Jumaane Williams, also running for the Democratic nomination for Governor, and his supporters in the Working Families Party also appear to be aware of the importance of the Latino vote, as they recruited Ana Maria Archila to run for Lieutenant Governor as Williams' running-mate. (Candidates for governor and lieutenant governor are not linked on the primary ballot, but they often present themselves to voters as running-mates.)

Will Latinos play a key role in who wins the governorship this year? Will Latinos defy previous voting patterns and turn out to vote in larger numbers?

The answer to the first question is a clear yes. The second question is more complicated, and my answer will come in the form of a challenge.

According to my analysis of voter rolls, Latinos are currently 18% of the entire state Democratic electorate, with 1,152,950 voters across the Empire State. This 18% represents the largest share of Latino Democratic voters in state history. Of the 1.15 million Latino voters, 862,255 are in New York City. That is a whopping 75% of the Latino electorate in the five boroughs.

Hence, any statewide candidate who does not visit the storefront cuchifritos in East Harlem or devour the excellent mangus at establishments in Washington Heights and the Bronx or stop by the taquerias in Sunset Park and visit the tree-lined streets of Corona and Elmhurst, will do so at their own peril.

Voter registration numbers, however, are not necessarily the equivalent of voting power. Voting power for Latinos will come once Latinos recognize that proper political representation and adequate policy attention to their plight can only come through robust and consistent voting participation.

As for proper representation, its lack is evident given the fact that among state legislators in New York City, only 17% are Latino, though Latinos represent 29% of the entire city population.

While Latinos continue to increase in the voting population, the fact remains that only 14% of the entire Democratic electorate in the last gubernatorial primary was Latino. To be sure, the low turnout rates among Latinos is not a dilemma unique to New York, as I have mentioned here before.[3] Yet the dilemma is here and must be dealt with.

On a more positive note, that 14% in 2018 was an increase compared to previous years, and even more importantly, since that last gubernatorial primary, Latino voting participation in New York City has already increased by 4% in the 2020 and 2022 primaries.

If the patterns of the last few years continue, I can foresee a scenario in which close to 250,000 Latinos could turn out statewide to vote in this June's Democratic primary. This would represent the largest ever turnout among Latinos in New York.

What can contribute to this potential increase of Latino voters?

One potential for increased Latino voting participation could lie in the fact that there could be two Latinas on the ballot for lieutenant governor, Reyna and Archila. Having two Latinas vying for the same position—against incumbent Lt. Gov. Brian Benjamin—may not be the most conducive to success for their respective candidacies. Such a scenario pits two Latinas against each other, potentially splitting the Latino vote for this position. Yet the Archila and Reyna candidacies can be a potential boon for Latino voting participation, provided that their campaigns invest enough resources (money, time, personnel) in Latino communities.

Archila's and Reyna's candidacies could be a bigger boost for Latino voters than the candidates at the top of the ballot—expected to include Hochul, Suozzi, and Williams, to name the top tier.

Previous studies point to increased voting among Latinos when viable Latino candidates are on the ballot. The well-respected Latino political scientist Matt Barreto, with Mario Villareal and Nathan Woods for instance, have studied Latino voting patterns in high density Latino precincts in California[4] and observed that the highest Latino turnout rates in Los Angeles occurred when a Latino was at the top of the ballot for mayor, both within the nonpartisan primaries and in the general elections.

I have used an analysis like Barreto's to investigate Latino voting patterns in New York and have also found that Latino voting participation has increased when a viable Latino has been at the top of the ballot.

---

3. Valentin, "Closer Look at New York City Latino Voter Participation."
4. Barreto et al., "Metropolitan Latino Political Behavior."

When observing Fernando Ferrer's candidacy for mayor of New York City in 2001, I noted an increase in voter participation within the New York precincts with the highest Latino populations in comparison with other mayoral primaries when a viable Latino was not on the ballot. In fact, voter participation in heavily Latino precincts increased an average of 30–40% in 2005, when Ferrer became the first Latino to win a Democratic mayoral primary, compared to years with no Latino candidate at the top of the ballot.

While the position of lieutenant governor is not atop the ballot, it still is a position of importance (though not so much in the day-to-day practical operations of state government), as is evident in the Cuomo saga and the eventual rise of Kathy Hochul to the governorship. This election cycle may be the first time that viable Latino candidates will appear on the ballot for a statewide position. And for this reason, provided that the Williams-Archila and Suozzi-Reyna tickets invest in the Latino vote, there is real potential for an increase in Latino voting participation.

What role might the Kathy Hochul-Brian Benjamin ticket have in bringing out the Latino vote this June? Up to this point, I have not seen the necessary investment on the part of Governor Hochul or the state Democratic Party apparatus in the Latino vote as a possible motivating factor for an increase in Latino voting participation. Outside of a few Latino appointments[5], and some holdovers from the Cuomo administration, Governor Hochul has not done much to increase Latino representation in state government.

At the time of this writing, only 5 of the 16 Latino New York City based state legislators have endorsed Hochul's candidacy.[6] Only two Latino New York City Council members have endorsed Hochul. And I have already noted how the state Democratic Party snubbed Latinos at its recent convention.

It may take two Latinas—Archila and Reyna—to help wake the sleeping giant that is the Latino vote in New York. It will of course take many others to contribute to the rise of Latinos in New York, but perhaps a lot more rests upon the shoulders of Archila and Reyna than they might think.

---

5. Lewis, "Hochul Adds More Latinos to Her Administration."
6. KathyHochul.com, "Endorsements."

20

The Pragmatic Progressivism
of Ritchie Torres

As CONGRESSIONAL REPRESENTATIVES SEEK re-election this year, there is one member of Congress who doesn't need to worry about having an opponent: Rep. Ritchie Torres. At the time of this writing, there is no word of a candidate circulating petitions to challenge Torres in this June's Democratic primary. As political insiders well know, it is rare for an incumbent in New York not to have a challenge.

Many may have taken notice of Torres's popularity in his congressional district, as is evident in this Data for Progress poll.[1] According to the poll, Torres enjoys a 73% favorability rate in the 15th Congressional District.

The rise of Ritchie Torres is one that I foresaw in these pages some[2] years ago. I believe the rest of the country will continue to share our New York experience of Torres as a thoughtful legislator who has an uncanny ability to dig through complex policy issues and who articulates his positions clearly and concisely. Equally fascinating to me has been Torres' political philosophy since 2013, a posture of pragmatic progressivism. The "pragmatic" part of this posture has earned Torres the scorn of some other progressives.

---

1. Data for Progress, "Ritchie Torres is Popular with NY-15."
2. Valentin, "Future of Latino Politics in New York City."

Contemporary political progressivism in the United States has several variants. The current trajectory of progressive politics can perhaps be distinguished between those on the socialist left and those on the liberal left, who consider themselves more pragmatic.

By "pragmatic" I am not referring to the philosophical school of thought of pragmatism made popular by the likes of William James and John Dewey in the 20th century. Rather, I refer to "pragmatic" as an electoral and governing approach to politics that seeks to achieve social ends through the most practical means possible.

These two distinguishing markers of political progressivism–the socialist left and the liberal left– are hardly a recent phenomenon. Since the 20th century, progressive politics has been quite diverse. Interestingly enough, the socialist left once had a similar influence in New York and national politics to what it has now, though the impact is perhaps a bit greater now if we consider the number of socialists that are being elected to local office. The recent electoral successes of socialists are due to their intentional efforts to work within the Democratic Party instead of functioning as a third party as they did decades ago.

Perhaps the most prominent and influential socialist figure in 1930s electoral politics was Norman Thomas, a member of the Socialist Party of America. Thomas' charm, charisma, and intellect helped to catapult the socialist agenda into the national political discourse.

Yet this socialist influence began to wane with the social progress achieved through FDR's New Deal initiatives. What replaced it for the next few decades was the influence of the liberal left.

What has been deemed "liberal left" I call pragmatic progressivism. And it is in this wing of progressive politics that Ritchie Torres resides. Pragmatic progressives seek most of the same goals as other progressives: universal healthcare, adequate funding for education and housing, fair wages, among others. The "pragmatic" element in this type of progressivism acknowledges that to function, politics must maintain a healthy equilibrium between competing interests.

The key difference between the socialist left and pragmatic progressives lies in the paths they take to achieve progressive aims. Pragmatists assert that the attainment of progressive goals may entail negotiating with those competing interests that are at different points along the political spectrum. Therefore, pragmatists make no bones about the fact that they must work within an imperfect and indeed broken system full of people with different opinions and constituencies that make these negotiations necessary. Pragmatists see these negotiations as necessary for the work of progress.

If Norman Thomas was the face of the socialist politics that preceded current socialist movements, like the contemporary Democratic Socialists of America (DSA), then the theologian and ethicist Reinhold Niebuhr, in the same era, represented the pragmatic progressivism exemplified today by Ritchie Torres.

In the 1930s, Niebuhr was part of the Socialists of America party and even ran for office twice on their ballot. The realities of World War II and the social and economic impact of FDR's New Deal changed his politics, leading him eventually to co-found New York's Liberal Party and later the Union for Democratic Action, which eventually became the Americans for Democratic Action. Niebuhr understood that the seeking of political perfection was far from realistic; therefore the necessity to seek compromise. He believed that the idealism of the socialist left, as was evident by their propensity to clamor for pacifictic alternatives during World War II, was indeed an attempt to seek the perfect. Yet, Niebuhr would assert that the perfect can't be the enemy of the very good.

Torres reflects in word and deed the type of progressive politics espoused by Niebuhr—seeking progressive goals by balancing realities of politics and governance.

When have we seen Rep. Torres' inclination toward this kind of pragmatic progressivism? Let's take a look at his stance on the "Defund the Police" movement prominently espoused by those on the socialist left. Speaking to Jose Diaz-Balart on MSNBC last month, Torres said, ". . . any elected official who's advocating for the abolition and/or even the defunding of police is out of touch with reality and should not be taken seriously."[3] Torres prefers to speak of a "reform the police" type of movement, one that acknowledges the necessity of policing for ensuring public safety while acknowledging also that there are structural deficiencies within police departments that need deep and sustained reform. Torres says, "What most New Yorkers want is not less policing or more police, but better policing—more accountable and transparent policing."[4]

Perhaps this stance of Torres's points to his inclination to work within a broken system in order to seek necessary changes from within rather than

---

3. Meyer, "Rep. Ritchie Torres Declares 'Defund the Police' Dead in NYC."
4. Cook et al., "Congressman Ritchie Torres on NYC Shootings."

seeking a total abolition of a system that doesn't work for many, particularly for communities of color. Hence, Torres has developed positions and backed legislation that seek to attack root causes of crime like poverty and housing instability, and pursues policies to address them.

Torres' position on the "Defund the Police" movement and his penchant for reforming systems from within deficient structures could perhaps be seen in a police reform bill fight in 2017, during his tenure in the New York City Council.

The 2017 Right to Know Act, a controversial and much-debated set of police reform bills, sought to deter police abuse and to ensure transparency in any interaction between an officer and an individual.

There were two bills in the Act, one introduced by then-City Council member and now Brooklyn Borough President Antonio Reynoso and the other introduced by Torres. After hearings and negotiations, Torres made changes to his bill. The Reynoso bill was championed by many police reform advocates, earning the praise of Monifa Bandele, a spokesperson for a prominent coalition, since Reynoso's bill would bring "transparency and accountability regarding searches during non-emergency policing encounters that have no legal basis other than a person's supposed consent."[5]

Of Torres' bill, Bandele said: "This NYPD bill being advanced by Torres is neither the Right to Know Act nor a compromise, but political backroom dealing and a surrender of legislative independence to the NYPD and the Mayor."[6] Bandele's statement reflected the sentiment of other reform advocates, who felt that the updated version of Torres' police reform bill conceded too much to the NYPD.

Torres indeed negotiated particulars of the bill with NYPD representatives and the mayor's office. But he insisted that any concessions made to the de Blasio administration would ensure the needed transparency in a number of interactions between police and individuals.

Torres earned the scorn of both police reform advocates and the police unions. History has shown that this type of criticism from both extremes is often the result of political decisions made by pragmatic progressives. Acknowledging the need for negotiations between disparate political interests and views in order to achieve progress on behalf of the citizenry never earns them friends at the extremes and most devoted parties, but does win them broad support among the more pragmatic general population.

5. Skelding, "Police Reform Group Accuses Torres of Surrender on Right to Know."
6. Skelding, "Police Reform Group Accuses Torres of Surrender on Right to Know."

Torres has done this again with his position on the status of Puerto Rico, siding for statehood for the Caribbean island, a position favored by conservatives on both the island and the mainland. A little over two weeks after winning his congressional race in a historically majority-Latino (and Puerto Rican) congressional district that was once represented by Herman Badillo, Torres penned an op-ed declaring his support for Puerto Rico statehood.[7] His statehood stance can be succinctly captured by his declaration that "As Americans, we must speak out forcefully against the *de jure* disenfranchisement of our fellow citizens in Puerto Rico, for it represents a deep rot at the very core of American democracy, not to mention a manifestation of the very systemic racism against which millions have stood in protest."

Using the lens of systemic racism to critique the current status of Puerto Rico is in essence utilizing a progressive principle (the fight against systemic racism and the acknowledgement of Puerto Rico's colonial status) in order to stand on the side of statehood, a position long held by mostly conservatives in Puerto Rico.

This position places Torres on the opposite side of the issue from the other two Puerto Rican congressional representatives in New York City, Reps. Nydia Velázquez and Alexandria Ocasio-Cortez, both of whom have introduced the *Puerto Rico Self-Determination Act of 2021*. The bill seeks to give Puerto Ricans on the island the opportunity to finally determine their status through an elaborate process that would include publicly-financed elections and a convention with delegates elected by the Puerto Rican people. Torres believes that Puerto Ricans have already determined their will by a recent referendum in which voters selected statehood as their preferred option.

While the police reform bill and Torres' position on the status of Puerto Rico may cause some to question his progressive bona fides, it is also important to remember his championing of a myriad of progressive issues. For instance, Torres has introduced a bill that would require the Federal Home Loan Banks to drastically increase investments in affordable housing, community development, and small business lending. And of course, on the issue of public housing, few elected officials in New York have been as relentless and consistent on the need to revamp our public housing facilities through massive federal investment. More recently, Torres led a

---

7. Torres, "Puerto Rico is Not For Sale."

push[8], supported by Ocasio-Cortez, demanding that billions in funding be secured for public housing and rental assistance.

It is difficult to peg Torres solely on one end of even the progressive spectrum. Throughout his career as an elected official, Torres' positions have reflected the thinking of a pragmatist who acknowledges the need to balance interests for the greater goal of achieving progressive values.

8. Frey, "Torres Leads 120-Plus Lawmakers in Call to Shield Billions for Public Housing."

21

Road to the Lieutenant Governor's Office Runs Through the Barrios of New York

UNTIL RESULTS ARE OFFICIALLY released, who will win an election is uncertain. But right now, with less than a week until election night in this year's statewide primaries, one thing is quite certain: the next Democratic nominee for Lieutenant Governor will have a Latino name. And yes, that even includes Antonio Delgado, whose racial and ethnic identity has been the subject of much debate.[1]

The fact that Delgado, Ana Maria Archila, and Diana Reyna are the three Democratic candidates on the ballot for Lieutenant Governor speaks to the growing importance of Latinos in state politics. Indeed, with Latinos now forming almost 20% of all registered Democratic voters statewide, the Latino vote is not one to take for granted.

Governor Hochul evidently knows this, as she and the State Democratic Party recently launched the Nueva York Initiative. Jumaane Williams' campaign and the New York Working Families Party as a key organizational engine were instrumental in launching Archila's candidacy. And Tom Suozzi asked Reyna to be his running-mate.

Having two Latinas as Lieutenant Governor candidates can be a boon for Latino voting participation. Several studies have shown that having a

---

1. Archila, "The Question Isn't Whether Antonio Delgado is Latino."

Latino at the top of the ballot does improve voting participation among the group. This was certainly the case in New York City when Fernando Ferrer became the first Latino to win the mayoral nomination of a major political party here. Latino voting participation increased by almost 40% in many of the Latino-majority election districts in his 2005 bid for Gracie Mansion. While the Lieutenant Governor race is not at the top of the ballot, it is right below the top, and can still garner enough attention to make some voters pay attention.

Can the candidacies of Archila, Delgado, and Reyna help increase Latino voter turnout across the city and state?

It depends. Boosting Latino turnout encompasses a number of things, like investing precious candidate time and financial resources in Latino neighborhoods, speaking to voters on the ground and through the airwaves.

It means meeting Latinos where they are. Paying lip-service will no longer work. In recent elections, we have seen numerous Latinos abandon their loyalty to the Democratic Party. Latino voters pay attention. And many more are going to the polls.

It also means investing money in Spanish-language TV and radio stations, and local papers. To be sure, voters of all ethnicities expect and respond positively to personal interactions with candidates. That is especially the case with Latinos, who expect candidates to be uno de ellos/ellas ("one of us"). Latinos enjoy the interaction and the excitement that campaigns generate and want the issues they care about dealt with, from small businesses to education to public safety to affordable housing and more.

So far, the potential for excitement is largely missing in Latino communities across the city and state. With just under a week to go before primary election day, the three lieutenant governor candidates have a lot of work to do to generate more buzz among Latinos.

It appears that so far only Delgado has bought advertisements on the major Spanish-language TV stations. Naturally, paying for pricey commercials entails having a large campaign kitty. Delgado was able to transfer millions of dollars from his congressional campaign account and, as the governor's running-mate and current lieutenant governor, will have the most money of the three candidates and thus more resources than others to do so.

Of the three, Archila has the most endorsements[2] from Latino elected officials, with 14. Delgado[3] and Reyna[4] each have four. Voters are not entirely swayed by endorsements, but endorsements can matter and can mean access to fundraising sources and personnel to launch on-the-ground operations to speak directly to voters.

Such endorsements will be pivotal, especially for Archila. Up to now, Archila seems to be running a somewhat similar campaign to Dianne Morales' in last year's mayoral primary, in that she appears focused on establishing and fortifying her progressive base as opposed to focusing on appealing to Latinos. While this progressive base has made possible the creation of a much-needed multi-racial coalition, the coalition is mostly driven by a political philosophy not embraced by a good chunk of the Latino Democratic primary electorate, which is more moderate. Moreover, the majority of likely Latino primary voters are 55 years of age and over, and many of these voters tend to be less progressive than younger ones.

Nevertheless, Archila's story is one that can certainly appeal to a broad spectrum of Latino voters. Like many Latinos across the Empire State, Archila immigrated to the United States in her youth—she came from Colombia when she was 17 years old. Undeterred by the challenges immigrants face on a daily basis, she dedicated her life to advocacy, co-founding Make the Road New York, a pivotal group doing important immigrants rights work across the state, and launching efforts to combat economic and racial injustice. Archila became nationally known for directly confronting U.S. Senator Jeff Flake during the Supreme Court nomination process of Brett Kavanaugh.

Diana Reyna also has a narrative that can appeal to many Latinos. The daughter of Dominican immigrants, Reyna became the first Dominican woman to be elected to a government position in the state of New York when she ascended to the New York City Council. She then became a deputy borough president under then-Brooklyn Borough President Eric Adams. Yet, Reyna's lack of financial resources and her inability to identify and energize a natural base for her candidacy will likely lead her to defeat.

In the end, the Lieutenant Governor primary race will probably come down to Archila and Delgado. Delgado is formidable, not because he has a Latino surname, but because of his campaign war chest, his access to the

2. AnaMariaForNY.com, "Endorsements."

3. DelgadoForNY.com, "Endorsements."

4. Coltin, "Endorsements in the 2022 Democratic Primary for Lieutenant Govenor."

state Democratic Party apparatus and many allies in organized labor, and by virtue of currently holding the position, albeit one he has not held for much time, which comes with additional support from Governor Hochul.

Delgado's success or defeat may be determined by Hochul's coattails, or lack thereof. And when it comes to the Latino vote in New York, he will have a lot of work to do, particularly since 75% of the Latino vote will come from New York City. Delgado is from upstate and is largely an unknown entity, especially among Latinos, in New York City.

Does the road to Albany cross through the Latino barrios of New York? Perhaps. One thing is certain—the next Democratic nominee for Lieutenant Governor will have a name that is familiar in those same barrios.

22

Latino Vote '22
5 Assembly Primaries to Watch

THOUGH THE GOVERNOR AND lieutenant governor races are getting the most buzz this state election cycle, a number of state legislative races—both Assembly and State Senate—are also surprisingly competitive.

Five of those competitive races happen to be in Latino-majority or Latino-plurality Assembly districts of New York City: two in the Bronx, two in Queens, and one in Brooklyn. These are the five to watch as the Assembly primaries are decided on Tuesday, June 28:

THE BRONX

Jose Rivera has represented the 78th Assembly district in the Bronx since 2000, when he won a seat previously occupied by Roberto Ramirez. Prior to winning this seat in 2000, Rivera served on the New York City Council, and before that, a five-year stint in the New York State Assembly. (Disclaimer: I have informally advised Rivera on his campaigns.)

Rivera represents the last of a generation of pioneering Latino politicians that are in elected office. He rose to power in 1982[1] after defeating the incumbent Sean Walsh. This was a time of rapid demographic change in the Bronx as Puerto Ricans spread to areas beyond the South Bronx. Rivera

---

1. Lynn, "Bronx Minority Democrats Given Aid."

took on the powers-that-be of the time, mostly Irish and Italian, and after years of organizing, won his seat exactly 40 years ago.

Now, Rivera has a fight on his hands as he seeks to fend off challenges from George Alvarez and Emmanuel Martinez.

Alvarez has the support of Congressman Adriano Espaillat and this endorsement has led to that of two others—Bronx City Council Members Oswald Feliz and Pierina Sanchez. By strategically endorsing Alvarez, it is clear that Espaillat is attempting to solidify his hold in the West Bronx, opting to depart from the unwritten rule of incumbents supporting other incumbents.

Martinez, who served as chairperson of Community Board 7 in the Bronx and was also elected a Democratic State Committee member, has received the support of the Moving NY Forward PAC, which is largely funded by a wealthy hedge-funder who, according to the Albany Times Union, is the "co-founder of a secretive Wall Street firm."[2]

The Alvarez and Martinez challenges are the toughest Rivera has faced in years. Yet Rivera has a solid and loyal base, is a formidable campaigner, and is known to frequent events with his ever-present camera on hand. Labor unions and the Bronx Democratic Party are solidly behind him, and Mayor Eric Adams has now endorsed Rivera too.

Moving northeast in the Bronx, the 82nd Assembly district is also home to an intense primary race. Assemblymember Michael Benedetto faces a strong challenge from Jonathan Soto.

Benedetto has served in office since 2004. The demographics of the 82nd district have changed significantly over the last two decades, and that district now has a Latino plurality. Among the Democratic electorate, Latinos make up 45% of all voters and their turnout has been consistent over the years. Evidence of this demographic change is Marjorie Velazquez's City Council victory last year. The 82nd Assembly district represents 54% of Velazquez's district, and Velazquez won her race handily, including in the 82nd Assembly district portion of the district. In this district, however, Latino votes alone will not push Soto to the victory line. Black and white voters are a significant chunk of the electorate, and to win a candidate will need to form a multi-racial coalition.

Alexandria Ocasio-Cortez's PAC, the Working Families Party, and other progressive groups are backing Soto. He is also receiving support

2. Bragg and Ward, "Longshot Assembly Candidates Faced a Mogul's Millions."

from the Move NY Forward PAC mentioned above. Soto is charismatic, whip-smart, and presents Benedetto's biggest challenge yet.

QUEENS

In Queens, two Assembly districts are ones to watch in terms of the Latino vote—the 30th and the 35th.

As a result of Assemblymember Brian Barnwell's decision not to seek re-election, the 30th Assembly district is an open seat and pits Steven Raga, a former Barnwell aide and a Filipino, against Ramon Cando, a Latino of Ecuadorian descent.

The district's demographic makeup in many ways represents the diversity that is Queens. Of the potential Democratic electorate there, 29% is Latino, 24% Asian, and 22% white. Several voter data experts (including the renowned Jerry Skurnik), deem another quarter of Democratic voters in that district as "other" since modeled demographic data cannot precisely match their ethnicities. Interestingly enough, when factoring in voting participation, the ethnic makeup of the voters remains the same; no particular ethnic group dominates when it comes to turnout.

The Queens Democratic Party apparatus and a number of labor groups are supporting Raga, but for some reason Barnwell, his former boss, is not. Cando is supported by Rep. Tom Suozzi, City Council Member Robert Holden, and Hiram Monserrate's Democratic club. While Raga has received critical establishment support, Cando's seeming support among Latinos and white voters appears to make him formidable.

Cando has presented himself as a more moderate "common sense" Democrat, eschewing the "defund" movement to divest police funding for community investments that Raga has espoused. Election day will demonstrate whether message trumps establishment support in this district.

In the 35th Assembly district, Monserrate is taking on the incumbent, Jeff Aubrey, in a rematch of 2020. Aubrey won that race but Monserrate is presenting a formidable challenge in what is a Latino plurality district. Latinos are 43% of the Democratic electorate, compared to 21% of the electorate that is Black and 9% that is Asian.

While Monserrate will always have to contend with his controversial and criminal past, his support among many Latinos in the district remains solid, and his Democratic club is a formidable force, having helped to elect other candidates in East Elmhurst and Corona.

Aubrey has the support of the Queens Democratic organization, in addition to numerous elected officials in surrounding districts, many who are mobilizing behind him and, sometimes more so, in opposition to Monserrate. Aubrey also has been able to maintain the support of a large number of African American voters who have been in the Elmhurst neighborhood for many years.

BROOKLYN

Brooklyn is also experiencing primary rumbles of particular significancee to the Latino vote, in this case in the 54th Assembly district. Progressive Samy Nemir Olivares is challenging Assemblymember Erik Dilan, son of former State Senator Martin Dilan, who lost to a progressive challenger himself in the 2018 primary when he was defeated by now-Senator Julia Salazar.

The two Latina congressional representatives in New York, Alexandria Ocasio-Cortez and Nydia Velazquez, are backing Nemir Olivares, as is Senator Salazar, the Working Families Party, the Democratic Socialists of America-New York City, and other progressive individuals and groups. By beating Tommy Torres for the district leader position, Nemir Olivares has already shown an ability to take on the Brooklyn machine and win.

This race is a particularly interesting one as a new test of the progressive-moderate split under the latest larger political context. Perhaps the race can show glimpses of where some Latino voters stand on the ideological spectrum, particularly in an area of the city where progressives have been on the rise but not necessarily because of the Latino vote. When Salazar defeated Martin Dilan in 2018, he won the most votes in the 54th Assembly district portion of the Senate district. Will the last vestiges of the Dilan dynasty fall? We're about to find out.

23

The Forgotten History of Latino Politics in New York

TUESDAY, JUNE 28, 2022, marked an important shift in Latino politics in New York, represented in part by Assemblymember Jose Rivera's Democratic primary loss to George Alvarez. The significance of Rivera's defeat goes beyond an election loss by someone who has been in office for four decades. Rivera represents the last of what can be deemed a third generation of Puerto Rican Latino elected officials, someone who was part of a generation that paved the way for the younger generation of current Latino political leaders.

Many of these younger leaders and members of the city's broader Latino communities may have little understanding of the significance of Rivera's life and career. This lack of historical perspective, important for understanding the trajectory of Latino politics in New York, one filled with long and difficult struggle, was made evident to me in a conversation I had with one leader who expressed bewilderment when I mentioned that Fernando Ferrer was the first Latino to win the Democratic nomination for the mayoralty in New York. The young leader had no idea who Ferrer was.

Rivera's loss represents yet another confirmation of a gargantuan historical and demographic shift taking place in Latino politics in New York. To understand how we, as Latinos, have arrived at this point, we must have perspective on, and appreciation of, the events and people that led us here.

The need to tell our political story as Latinos has been burning inside me for years and has only intensified since that conversation with the young leader last year, in light of Dianne Morales' run for the mayoralty, debate over representation at the statewide level amid two lieutenant governor vacancies, and other recent developments.

The following presents an outline of what has become a book I am writing on the history of Latino politics in New York. Rivera's defeat, like his victory over an Irish incumbent 40 years ago, has a history. And it must be told. Here's a snapshot of it.

PUERTO RICAN MIGRATION, CIGAR MAKERS, AND NUMBERS RUNNERS, OH MY!

The history of Latino politics in New York is largely the history of Puerto Rican politics in New York. Though a new chapter in this history has been emerging, the fact remains that up until 1991, when Guillermo Linares became the first Dominican elected in the history of New York, almost all Latino elected officials in New York were Puerto Ricans.

The long and difficult struggle for Latino political representation begins 100 years ago with an unlikely cast of characters: cigar makers and numbers runners. By the mid-1920s, a large number of Puerto Ricans began to arrive on the shores of Gotham City. This first spurt of Puerto Rican migration was a direct result of the passage of the Jones Act in 1917, which forced on the island of Puerto Rico economic consequences that are still being felt today.[1] Eight years after the Jones Act, an additional 40,000 Puerto Ricans arrived in New York, drastically increasing the community's overall population from a mere 2,000 just a little over a decade before.

Most workers in the early Puerto Rican labor force were cigar-makers populating factories all over the city, including those like El Morito on 86th Street and 3rd Avenue in Manhattan, a location now surrounded by luxury high-rises and about a half-mile from East Harlem, which would become one of the early hubs of the Puerto Rican community.

The cigar-makers (tabaqueros) were a learned bunch. Bernardo Vega, one of the first to chronicle his life as a Puerto Rican migrant in New York post-1917, describes the type of colleagues he encountered at El Morito. There was Juan Hernandez, director of the workers' paper, and Enrique Rosario Ortiz, Tomas Perez, and Matias Nieves, whom he describes as people

---

1. Denis, "The Jones Act: The Law Strangling Puerto Rico."

active in the worker cause and in the wider Latino community. With such outstanding workers, it is no surprise to read from Vega that they hired lectors to read to all the workers for an hour in the morning and an hour in the afternoon. Morning reading sessions were devoted to the latest news of the day. Afternoon readings were headier and included political and literary tomes.

The tabaqueros were not only learned, they were also extremely organized. These organizational abilities and structures are what eventually led to political recognition. The tabaqueros were instrumental in fighting for workers' rights, fair wages, and fair labor practices. They organized a number of small strikes, which culminated in a bigger strike in 1919.

While the 1919 strike did not necessarily lead to improved conditions, employers and others could not ignore the tabaqueros—these Latino men (overwhelmingly Puerto Rican) were brilliant, conscious of their own value (as Puerto Ricans and as a labor force) and highly organized. Many took notice, including an Italian-American politician who would eventually become mayor of New York City, Fiorello LaGuardia.

Interestingly, many of these tabaqueros were socialists, including Bernardo Vega and Jesus Colon, another key figure in early Latino politics in New York. The workers' cause became an impetus for embracing socialist principles, which Puerto Ricans in New York had brought with them from the island.

All this led Bernardo Vega to initiate the first Puerto Rican chapter of the Socialist Party in New York. Other prominent early groups, like the Alianza Obrera Puertorriqueña, became hubs for the gathering of Puerto Rican socialists. One fascinating fact about the early Puerto Rican socialists is that they believed in the necessity of coalition-building for the cause of economic justice. Thus these same groups invited over 200 Jewish socialists to partake in conversations around workers' struggles both in Puerto Rico and New York.

Indeed, Rep. Alexandria Ocasio-Cortez's socialist background has deep roots in early Puerto Rican politics in New York.

Puerto Ricans arriving in New York began to realize that in New York they would also face poor economic conditions, though perhaps not as severe as the conditions they had left behind. The economic struggles made early efforts to organize politically a daunting task. Effective organizing meant proper funding. Where would an economically struggling community turn?

Besides the tabaqueros, numbers runners (boliteros) were pivotal in what would become the early efforts in Latino politics in New York. The boliteros were among the early financial backers of the first Puerto Rican political clubs and organizations. One of these boliteros was Carlos Tapia, whom Nestor David Pastor would describe as the Puerto Rican Luke Cage.[2] Tapia, with his linebacker size, was instrumental in the struggle for political empowerment and in defending Puerto Ricans against racism and police brutality. He would go on to co-found one of the very early Puerto Rican Democratic clubs in New York, the Betances Democratic Club in Brooklyn.

Tapia owned his own bodegas and restaurants and would go on to push these same clubs and organizations to cease receiving funding from the boliteros. By that point, in the late 1920s and early 1930s, Puerto Rican political organizations had garnered enough experience and channeled enough energy to gain the attention and support of some of the Democratic County organizations in the city.

Right alongside, and often in front of, these men were pioneering Puerto Rican women who also dedicated their lives to the social and political empowerment of Puerto Ricans. Noteworthy among these women is Antonia Denis. Unfortunately, not much information remains about Denis' life and work.

All of the early pioneers are gone and very little documentation remains of the efforts of Denis and others. What we do know is that Denis was instrumental in the start of the Betances club as well as other political and cultural organizations and that she was known to be a one-woman voter registration and voter turnout champion.

Denis also was a pivotal figure in the early efforts to commemorate Puerto Rican culture and contributions through cultural festivities like the Puerto Rican Day parade. Fortunately, some audio recordings of interviews exist at the Center for Brooklyn History[3]; they document Denis' work, and she can be deemed the first instrumental Puerto Rican woman in Latino politics in New York.

The fruitful efforts of the early political organizing efforts, coupled with the continued increase in the Puerto Rican population of New York, would lead to actual political representation. It was a slow and gradual process, but by 1937 these efforts would lead to the election of the first Latino elected in the history of New York, Puerto Rican Oscar Garcia Rivera.

2. Pastor, "Carlos Tapia, The Puerto Rican Luke Cage of the Brooklyn Waterfront."
3. Center for Brooklyn History Finding Aids, "Guide to the Antonia Denis Collection."

Garcia Rivera, a St. John's Law School graduate, would go on to serve in the State Assembly, representing the 17th Assembly District in East Harlem, now the 68th District.

24

The Forgotten History of Latino Politics in New York: Part II

THE REPUBLICAN PARTY DURING the pre-FDR era was surely not the GOP of today, in New York and beyond. This is made clear by who the Republicans chose as their candidate for State Assembly in what was then considered "South Harlem."

Oscar García Rivera was by no means a Republican as we understand the term today; he had not a single conservative bone in his body. In fact, Garcia Rivera was a true progressive through and through. For supporters like the cigar-makers (see part one of this column[1]), it was easy to rally behind one of their own, for he was not only a Puerto Rican, he was also a socialist.

As is typical of any winning campaign, especially one looking to unseat an incumbent, García Rivera's victory in 1937 was a result of a confluence of support from leaders and organizations and the right political climate—a climate that increasingly demanded broader representation.

On one hand, after a decade of ardent struggle for representation in which the number of Puerto Ricans in New York continued to rise, nationalist fervor among Puerto Ricans in Gotham was palpable by the time García Rivera sought the Assembly seat in East Harlem. On the other hand,

1. Valentin, "The Forgotten History of Latino Politics in New York."

long-standing progressives saw an opportunity to elect someone who aligned with their progressive values. Thus, staunch Marxists, labor activists, the American Labor Party, and the city's Fusion Party, together with the burgeoning Puerto Rican electorate and a Republican Party looking to defeat a Democrat, were part of a grand coalition that made possible the election of the first Latino in New York.

The prospect of electing "one of their own" was widespread among Puerto Ricans, even in areas outside of East Harlem. La Prensa, one of the first Spanish-language dailies in New York (La Prensa would merge with El Diario de Nueva York to form El Diario/La Prensa in 1963), wrote several articles on García Rivera's campaign. One such article comes across as rather mundane—"Aumenta el interés en la campaña en el Distrito No. 17." The piece highlights a "gran mitin" (a great meeting) that brought together the coalition rallying around García Rivera. Even the Spanish-language reporters, who perhaps in this instance relinquished some impartiality, could not contain their glee at the possibility of electing the first Puerto Rican not only in New York but also in the continental United States.

However, García Rivera's appealing candidacy was a threat to the powers of the time and was met with strong opposition, most notably from the powerful Tammany Hall machine. Their candidate was the incumbent, Meyer Alterman, a Democrat who was also the chairman of the powerful Ways and Means Committee in the Assembly. One of the Spanish-language dailies reported on some of Tammany Hall's typical shenanigans, including fraudulent voter registrations in order to cast illegal votes.

Responding to one of the Spanish-language dailies' inquiry into an increase in voter registration ahead of the election, García Rivera himself noted that Tammany Hall Democrats via the Wichita and Owasco Democratic clubs, made a concerted effort to hamper Latino voter registration by providing false information to eligible Puerto Rican voters. In some cases, these Tammany Hall loyalists told Puerto Ricans that they were obligated to take a first-time voter exam in Brooklyn, when this was not the case. In other cases, Tammany Hall made sure to fraudulently pad voter rolls by registering non-Latino individuals in specific Latino households. By García Rivera's own estimates, out of a total of 6,000 newly-registered voters ahead of the election, at least 2,000 were fraudulent registrants.

It was clear that Tammany Hall would use all their influence, including strong-handed and illegal tactics to deter the first Latino from winning a seat in the Assembly.

Yet, demographic destiny was on García Rivera's side. Coupled with the support of Mayor Fiorello La Guardia, who ran on the same ticket as Thomas Dewey in his 1937 race for district attorney, and the fierce support of labor leaders like David Dubinsky, Alex Rose, and Mike Quill, García Rivera would go on to defeat the incumbent by more than 1,500 votes in an election that saw 17,807 voters go to the polls.

García Rivera understood right away that his historic election was in part a result of the people's desire for a change from the conventional political misconduct. He was not, and never would be, indebted to Tammany Hall Democrats. His allegiance was to the people and the people alone.

East Harlem was also a community in great need—East Harlemites clamored for political leadership that would fight to alleviate the ills plaguing it, from rampant poverty to a housing affordability crisis. They hoped García Rivera would do his part in the Assembly. And that he did.

When asked by La Prensa's Antulio Rodriguez Castillo what legislative agenda he would take to Albany, García Rivera responded straightforwardly, clearly showing that the progressive philosophy he ran on was not mere rhetoric, but rather stemmed from a deep belief that a progressive agenda was exactly what would benefit the poor of East Harlem.

García Rivera's first order of business was to introduce an affordable housing bill that aimed to restrict the ability of landlords to raise rents arbitrarily. It is rather ironic that 85 years after García Rivera's election, East Harlem and indeed the city as whole face a major housing affordability crisis (and there is fierce debate over a bill in Albany that would cap rent increases).

García Rivera also sought to root out the corruption prevalent in city politics, which he felt contributed to the crises plaguing areas like East Harlem. Perhaps his idealistic views about what good government could do were balanced with some political realism—taking on corruption in government would continue to help weaken an already declining Tammany Hall, which would surely help his re-election efforts.

García Rivera promised to work with Mayor La Guardia's administration and newly-elected Manhattan District Attorney Dewey, to root out corruption in government. According to García Rivera, Dewey, who would later become governor and the Republican nominee for president in 1948, promised to work with him on such efforts. It could be said that Dewey lived up to his promises since he went on to prosecute Tammany Hall boss James Joseph Hines on racketeering charges.

García Rivera was successfully re-elected in 1938. His second winning political campaign was not just a result of the debilitation of Tammany Hall; García Rivera also had a solid record to run on.

In just one year, he introduced a number of bills supported by progressives. More importantly, these bills were seen as a powerful message to the people of East Harlem that their community finally had an elected leader that prioritized their needs and not those of Tammany Hall. García Rivera introduced an anti-discrimination bill that would fine employers for refusing to pay workers because of race. In 1938 he introduced a civil rights bill (almost 30 years before the passage of the 1965 federal Voting Rights Act), and as promised, he introduced the aforementioned legislation that would limit the right of landlords to raise rents arbitrarily. In an address to residents in his community, García Rivera said the bill would be a "deterrent to greedy landlords" and would "protect the tenants in the low income bracket."

With this record, García Rivera was ready for his re-election battle. This time, however, his enemies were not just limited to Tammany Hall Democrats. The Republican County organization, which had backed him just one year earlier, denied García Rivera the nomination in 1938 (Assembly elections were yearly then). The New York Times called it "an unusual political move." García Rivera likened it to yet another Tammany Hall hit job.

Irvin Levy, the Republican leader in García Rivera's district, told the Times that their support was rescinded because of García Rivera's supposed closeness to communists. The GOP instead lent their support to a young African-American attorney by the name of John A. Ross. The Tammany Hall Democrats supported Meyer Alterman again, leaving García Rivera as the third-party candidate of the American Labor Party. Democrats and Republicans alike thought they had García Rivera's number. The result was a nail-biter but García Rivera ended up victorious, besting Alterman by 235 votes.

Two years later, dynamics would shift drastically for García Rivera and the burgeoning East Harlem Puerto Rican community. Redistricting efforts significantly altered the 17th Assembly district and as a result, Democrat Hulan Jack beat García Rivera by 3,150 votes in 1940. García Rivera's defeat also spelled temporary doom for Puerto Rican representation, as no Latinos were elected to any office for more than a decade.

Interestingly enough, during this void in Puerto Rican political representation a non-Puerto Rican, Congressman Vito Marcantonio, would go on to champion the cause of Puerto Ricans in New York and those on the Caribbean island.

The lack of Latino political representation after García Rivera's defeat was not a reflection of any decline in the Latino population of New York. In fact, the very opposite was occurring. As the '40s gave way to the '50s, the growing number of Puerto Ricans in New York would increase by over 300%, from a little under 60,000 in 1940 when García Rivera was defeated to almost 300,000 by 1950. These New York City statistics in all likelihood underestimate the real picture of Puerto Rican migration at the time. By 1956, just six years later, an additional 300,000 Puerto Ricans had arrived in the city. (My parents were two of these 300,000; my father arrived in East Harlem in 1955 and my mother came to the same community in 1956.)

The continued rise of the Puerto Rican population meant that political machines could no longer bypass the need for Puerto Rican political representation. Much too large to ignore, the Puerto Rican population was ready to again elect one of its own.

In 1953, Felipe Torres, a 56-year-old attorney and graduate of Fordham Law School, was elected to the State Assembly, becoming the first Latino elected in the borough of the Bronx. Interestingly, the Torres family became prominent not only in political circles but also within the legal profession. After his stint in the Assembly, Felipe Torres was appointed a Family Court judge. His son Frank succeeded him in the Assembly and was also later appointed a judge. Felipe's granddaughter, Analisa Torres is currently a federal judge, appointed by Barack Obama in 2013. (I was honored to help Analisa Torres in 1998 during her successful run for Civil Court judge in Manhattan.)

By the time Felipe Torres was elected, there were more Puerto Ricans in the Bronx than in East Harlem. Yet, East Harlem was the place that Puerto Rican political power would flourish first. In 1954, the last of the Tammany Hall bosses, Carmine DeSapio, appointed Tony Mendez as a district leader in East Harlem. Thus, Mendez became the first Latino Democratic district leader in New York history. Twenty-four years later, in 1978, his daughter-in-law Olga Mendez became the first Latina elected to a State Legislature in U.S. history. Tony Mendez founded the Caribe Democratic Club, which remains in existence today and is headed by an East Harlem community activist, Raul Reyes.

Mendez knew how to work DeSapio in order to increase Puerto Rican representation at all levels of government. Largely through Mendez's efforts, Emilio Nunez, a member of his club, was elected to the City Court in 1956. Another Caribe Club member, Jose Ramos-Lopez was appointed to the Workmen's Compensation Board. Manuel Gomez became deputy commissioner in the Magistrate's Court. By the end of the decade, Ramos-Lopez was elected to the State Assembly, becoming the third Puerto Rican elected to the State legislature in New York history.

The advancement of Puerto Rican political power in East Harlem was a source of admiration for others around the city, particularly in the Bronx. However, East Harlem continued to get a bigger piece of the political pie, even though the Bronx constituted a larger portion of the Puerto Rican community in New York. Bronx political leaders called for greater representation, scorning their own political leaders, particularly Bronx Democratic boss Charles Buckley, for not doing more for the Puerto Rican community.

That would soon change in the 1960s when Herman Badillo entered the picture and became a political hero for Puerto Ricans in New York.

25

Latinos and the August 2022 New York State Senate Primary

LAST WEEK'S PRIMARY ELECTIONS for New York State Senate and U.S. House of Representatives seats included a number of competitive races, some of them in Latino-majority districts. As in any election, the implications of this primary are varied and significant.

Here are several key takeaways from State Senate races in the five boroughs.

LATINO TURNOUT, WHERE ART THOU?

Voter turnout at this primary was abysmal, as was widely predicted, but especially in Latino districts—as it had been in the June primaries for state-wide and Assembly seats.

According to my estimates based on voter enrollment analysis, of the 802,433 Latino registered Democratic voters in New York City, only 67,871 voted in the June primary. Yes, a paltry 8% of all eligible Latino Democratic voters went to the polls in those primaries, including the race for the party's Democratic nomination for Governor of New York. Granted, turnout was down across all racial and ethnic backgrounds from the 2018 jump. Yet, the most significant drop in voting participation is among Latinos, followed by

Asian American and African American voters, respectively, when comparing the 2018 and 2022 Democratic primaries for Governor.

As yet we have only *unofficial* results from this month's primary, with thousands of absentee ballots still being tallied. But these show that Latino turnout in the August primaries has decreased even more.

Take the 78th Assembly district in the Bronx as an example, where more than half of registered voters are Latinos. The district saw a highly-competitive Assembly Democratic primary in June, along with the statewide Democratic primaries for Governor and Lieutenant Governor

This month, that Assembly district largely overlapped with two competitive primaries at the State Senate level in the 31st and 33rd Senate districts. Combined, the two Senate districts include 49 of the 52 Election Districts that make up the 78th Assembly district. Both these Senate districts had competitive primaries.

The 78th Assembly district saw a turnout of 4,163 voters in the June primary, where longtime incumbent Assemblymember Jose Rivera was defeated by George Alvarez, and Governor Kathy Hochul and Lieutenant Governor Antonio Delgado each beat two Democratic opponents. Those 4,163 voters made for an almost 47% decline from the June 2021 New York City primary cycle, which featured the highly-competitive Democratic primaries for Mayor, Comptroller, and Bronx Borough President, as well as partially overlapping races in the 14th and 15th City Council Districts.

By my calculations, only 2,963 people turned out to vote this month in the 78th Assembly district in the Bronx (that number could increase very slightly with a small number of additional absentee ballots to be counted there).

Why are the numbers so abysmal? This year's redistricting fiasco, including a judge's decision to force an August primary, making for two primaries in the same cycle, contributes mightily to this decline. But there are other factors too, like an uninspiring gubernatorial primary, lack of Latino political leadership, rampant poverty, voter apathy, and more.

To understand these social and political realities among Latinos, I am launching a new think tank—The Institute for Latino Politics and Policy—during Hispanic Heritage Month, which is September 15-October 15. Stay tuned for more information.

The voting apathy in the 78th Assembly district is also found in other districts with large Latino voting populations. For the sake of all Latino communities, it is high time that Latino political and community leaders, community organizations, and others set aside their personal gripes and tribalism. Of course Latinos are not a monolithic community; we come from different countries, with nuances in our language, culture, politics, and ideologies. But surely there is more that connects us than divides us.

THE SENATE RACES

A number of this year's competitive New York State Senate races occurred in Latino-majority or Latino-plurality districts.

In the 31st Senate district, spanning parts of Upper Manhattan and the South Bronx, three insurgents took on the incumbent senator, Robert Jackson. But Jackson's toughest challenger was Angel Vasquez, who had the strong backing of Congressman Adriano Espaillat.

With the changes that resulted from the wacky redistricting process, the 31st Senate district experienced some radical shifts, and became much more Latino in the process. In fact, the Senate district was constructed in a way that resembles Rep. Espaillat's own Congressional district. The new demographic reality of the district was one that on paper would give someone like Vasquez a fighting chance to defeat the incumbent.

Alas, not only did Jackson win, he won handily. In fact, Jackson's performance was one of the most impressive of the night. He won all Assembly districts in the Senate district, except for one—the 86th Assembly district in the Bronx. And this is where it gets interesting.

Jackson defeated Vasquez in the 72nd Assembly district, which comprises 44% of the entire Senate district. In this district, 70% of all Democratic voters are Latino (overwhelmingly Dominican). And it is Espaillat's home base.

According to the unofficial results, Jackson won 50% of the vote in the 72nd Assembly district, to Vasquez's 42%. Jackson's impressive victory testifies to the vast support he receives from voters of all ethnic backgrounds. He is likable, known to be thoughtful, and was a progressive before it became the political buzzword of the day.

The results of the race have major implications for Espaillat, who was not on the ballot for State Senate but for Congress. Much was said, including by me, about Espaillat's ability to get his preferred candidates elected: Oswald Feliz and George Alvarez in the Bronx, Carmen De La Rosa and Manny De Los Santos in Manhattan, to name a few. Yet, in this case, Espaillat could not carry one of his own on his home turf. This fact alone makes

Espaillat one of the night's biggest losers. Interestingly enough, this comes on the heels of City and State listing him #1[1] on its "Manhattan Power 100" list. Of course, every great warrior lives to see another day. But this warrior has taken a major blow from another, Robert Jackson.

Another of Espaillat's endorsed candidates, Miguelina Camilo, lost her race to unseat State Senator Gustavo Rivera in the Bronx. Rivera's victory is another of the night's most impressive wins.

Not only was Rivera vastly outspent (outside groups alone spent over $1 million to defeat him), but other major forces were out to get him: the Bronx Democratic machine, the Dinowitz father-son elected tandem, Congressman Ritchie Torres, Bronx Borough President Vanessa Gibson, and other elected officials. Prominent labor unions DC37 and 32BJ also backed Camilo.

Despite these unusual odds for an incumbent, Rivera defeated Camilo, receiving 52% of the votes in the unofficial tally. As a result of Assemblymember Jose Rivera's defeat in the June primary, Senator Gustavo Rivera is to become the second most senior Latino elected representative in the Bronx, after Senator Jose Serrano.

Rivera's victory may also demonstrate further that the Bronx Democratic Party is more of a paper tiger than a machine. The fact is that over the years Democratic county organizations have lost much of the power they once had. They still have influence, but for the most part the victories of many insurgent candidates over machine-backed candidates in recent years demonstrate county organizations' waning power. Senator Rivera's victory continues to show that great candidates, with a strong and organized campaign operation to back them, and enough money to put it together, can defeat county organizations.

In the 34th Senate district, a district covering the Northeast Bronx and a sliver of Westchester, Assemblymember Nathalia Fernandez handily defeated two other candidates in an 'open' race to replace State Senator Alessandra Biaggi, who declined to run for reelection to unsuccessfully pursue a seat in Congress.

And in the 59th Senate district, which covers stretches of western Queens and Brooklyn and a chunk of Manhattan's East Side, newcomer Kristen Gonzalez defeated Elizabeth Crowley. Gonzalez, backed by the Democratic Socialist of America—New York City (DSA), also had to

---

1. City & State, "The 2022 Manhattan Power 100."

contend with the vast spending of outside forces. Yet, she won with an impressive 58% of the vote in the unofficial tally.

Gonzalez now joins Rep. Alexandria Ocasio-Cortez, State Senator Julia Salazar, Assemblymembers Jessica Gonzalez-Rojas and Marcela Mitaynes, and City Council Members Alexa Aviles and Tiffany Caban in the ranks of DSA-backed Latino elected representatives. While in some quarters the NYC DSA has been critiqued for its far-left positions on public safety and other topics, and questioned about the diversity in its leadership, it does overwhelmingly support candidates of color, particularly Latinos. Would it be a stretch to say that in some Latino-plurality districts there seems to be a return to electing Latino socialists? Or does this merely reflect the cyclical nature of politics? Maybe both. As I pointed out[2] in a recent column, and will develop in a forthcoming piece, the very first Latino elected official in our state's history was a socialist, Puerto Rican Oscar Garcia Rivera.

Lastly, despite abysmal turnout, the election of Latinas is a welcome breath of fresh air, and adds to overall Latino representation in the State Senate.

The new Fernandez and Gonzalez victories in their primaries (with an overwhelmingly Democratic electorate, both are all but assured of winning in the fall general election), combined with the virtually certain re-election of the other Latino senators—Jessica Ramos, Gustavo Rivera, Julia Salazar, Luis Sepulveda, Jose Serrano—will increase Latino representation in the Senate to at least seven.

A potential victory by Democratic nominee Monica Martinez on Long Island in November could increase Latino representation in the State Senate to eight in the 63-seat upper chamber of the Legislature. And five of the eight would be Latinas, with three of the five of Colombian descent—Nathalia Fernandez, Jessica Ramos, Julia Salazar. Now that's worth celebrating!

2. Valentin, "The Forgotten History of Latino Politics in New York."

26

Latinos, Hochul, and the 2022 Election for New York Governor

SHE ONCE ADAMANTLY OPPOSED the idea of giving drivers' licenses to undocumented immigrants; she even went so far as to threaten their arrests and deportations. No Latinos were on the original list of speakers for the convention of the State Democratic Party, of which she is the *de facto* leader. The *Nueva York Initiative* the party established as an effort to woo Latinos would, they said, only generate a "multi-year, six-figure investment." A paltry six-figure amount is not nearly enough to make a dent among Latino voters. Though a lieutenant governor with a Latino-sounding name was appointed, Antonio Delgado is not actually a Latino. And when new party executive leadership was selected not too long ago, no Latinos were on the list.

With an abysmal record on Latino matters, can Governor Kathy Hochul win the Latino vote in this year's election? The short answer is "yes—but." She may win their vote, but it'll likely be with a smaller margin than that of any of her Democratic predecessors.

Much has been said about the non-homogeneity of Latinos, and that is certainly true. Latinos come from a variety of Latin American countries, with differences in culture, language accents, and the like. Yet despite this wide-ranging diversity, Latinos in New York tend to vote Democratic and for the most part align on issues of importance. For example, a UCLA study[1] showed that 78% of Latinos in high Latino-density election districts in New York voted for Joe Biden in the 2020 presidential election.

At the statewide level, Latino voting preferences tend to follow the same Democratic line. By my own estimations, Andrew Cuomo's support among Latinos in his elections hovered between 62% and 65%. Most public polling data tended to show slightly lower levels of Latino support, as this Siena College poll[2] taken close to the 2018 election demonstrates.

Among the public polls that included Latinos in their crosstabs, Cuomo would tend to poll in the high 50s to low 60s. We must bear in mind that most public polls have a tendency of missing the mark on Latino support since they fail to correctly sample Latinos within their surveys. For instance, polls that undersample Latinos increase the margin of error in the Latino demographic and create particularly imprecise data.

These inaccuracies notwithstanding, Hochul has been polling at lower levels than Cuomo among Latinos. This October Siena poll[3] had Hochul at 56% among Latinos.

An October Marist poll[4] had Hochul at 55% with Latinos, where an October SurveyUSA poll[5] had Latino voter support for Hochul at 45% with an additional 19% of Latinos polling undecided. Again, despite the undersampling of Latinos, these Hochul numbers suggest that her level of support among Latinos is still lower than Cuomo's.

Yet I suggest that these Hochul numbers do not necessarily represent Latino defection from the Democratic Party or from Democratic candidates and thus a pull to embracing conservative candidates and ideologies. Current voter registration data does not suggest significant Latino defections from Democrats to Republicans. Furthermore, recent election results, like Eric Adams' victory last November, also do not show any evidence that Latino voters in New York City (75% of Latino voters statewide reside in the City of New York) are leaving the Democratic Party or its candidates

1. Domínguez-Villegas et al., "Vote Choice of Latino Voters in the 2020 Presidential Election."

2. Siena College Research Institute, "October 28–November 1, 2018; 641 New York State Likely Voters."

3. Siena College Research Institute, "Siena College Poll Conducted by the Siena College Research Institute."

4. https://maristpoll.marist.edu/wp-content/uploads/2022/10/Marist-Poll_NY-NOS-and-Tables_202210101405.pdf

5. https://www.surveyusa.com/client/PollReport.aspx?g=3b2816e1–9efc-4d5e-a219–3c3c9ab52993

in droves. Latino support for the Democrat Adams resembled support for previous Democratic mayoral candidates.

Furthermore, the recent polling on the 2022 general election may also bear this out. Latino support for Senator Chuck Schumer's reelection is at 57% (versus 45% for Hochul) in the SurveyUSA poll, 63% in the Siena poll (to 56% for Hochul). The Marist poll is the only public poll that has Hochul receiving a higher percentage of the Latino vote than Schumer (55–53%). When it comes to support for President Biden and Democratic congressional candidates, Latino support is consistently in the 60% range, also higher than Latino support for Hochul.

So, what gives with Hochul?

Several factors may account for Hochul's lower numbers among Latinos than her predecessor. On one hand, most public polls indicate that crime remains the key issue for Latino voters, more so than economic concerns. It may be the case that Latinos are not happy with Hochul's handling of crime, which typically hits communities of color harder than other demographic groups. Lee Zeldin, Hochul's Republican challenger, is running the typical GOP election playbook and hammering Hochul on the significant crime problem in New York.

Second, the lower level of Latino support may be a consequence of Hochul's election strategy, one which many have deemed an equivalent to the Rose Garden strategy made popular by William McKinley in the late 19th century and Jimmy Carter in the 20th. Hochul has refrained from the type of sustained retail politics that Latinos appreciate and by which they are motivated.

Lastly, Latinos may be getting tired of a political party that seemingly has only paid lip service to the needs and demands of its communities, from public safety and small businesses to education and housing. And even when the party and its leaders make attempts to reach into Latino neighborhoods, they respond with paltry attempts like that of the Nueva York Initiative and its minor "investment."

Yet, Latinos across the nation and in New York have consistently and faithfully pulled the levers for Democratic candidates, including Governor Hochul in June's Democratic primary. Many Latinos would say that they have not left the Democratic Party or its leaders; the party and its leaders have left the Latino constituency

Hochul has her work cut out for her in Latino neighborhoods across the state. The last two weeks of the race will be critical for her election efforts, particularly as campaigns shift into get-out-the-vote. Will Latinos see their governor?

27

A Sad Day for Latinos in New York
Hector LaSalle's Rejection

THE NEW YORK STATE Senate's Wednesday rejection of Justice Hector La-Salle's nomination for Chief Judge of the Court of Appeals, the state's highest court, is yet another example of how Latinos continuously get shafted. We can no longer say such dismissal is the fault of conservatives rather than progressives: lack of advancement for Latinos has truly become a nonpartisan affair. The shafting is equal opportunity, with Latinos consistently on the receiving end.

Like Governor Hochul's last major nominations—first the selection of Brian Benjamin and then, after Benjamin's resignation amid corruption charges, Antonio Delgado for lieutenant governor—the rollout of this pick has been riddled with problems from the outset.

The Delgado and LaSalle choices apparently recognized that Latinos are a group to be reckoned with. Yet, serious Hochul blunders plagued both selections.

Delgado has a Latino sounding name but is not actually Latino, much to the disappointment of Latinos across New York who have long clamored for representation at the highest levels of state government. LaSalle's nomination—which could have made him the first Latino Chief Judge in state history—resulted in a backlash from many progressive and some moderate elected officials and groups, as well as some labor unions. Hochul's inability to communicate with key stakeholders before a public announcement that she was going to nominate LaSalle is partly, though not entirely, to blame for this defeat.

There is no guarantee that another Latino candidate will be nominated, especially if the previous list of candidates presented by the state's Commission on Judicial Nomination is any indication.

The contentious battle spurred by this nomination has further exposed a shift that is occurring in Latino politics in New York: there is a crop of Latinos that were part of the early (and current) struggles for Latino representation at all levels of government and there is a newer generation of Latino leaders that see ideological fidelity as being as important as representation itself, if not more so.

In this LaSalle battle, Luis Miranda and Roberto Ramirez represent the protagonists of the first group, both long-time powerhouse lobbyists and political consultants. Miranda and Ramirez were architects of Fernando Ferrer's mayoral bids in the mid-2000s, and have more recently worked on Letitia James' successful run for state attorney general, among other campaigns.

Miranda and Ramirez organized a number of other Latino leaders, many of whom have long struggled for representation. There is Fernando Ferrer himself; Melissa Mark-Viverito, a progressive who made history as the first Latina to serve as speaker of the City Council; and former labor leader Dennis Rivera, among many others. Miranda and company know first-hand the importance of representation and have seen LaSalle's nomination as a necessary step for a group that has long been ignored, undervalued, and held back.

The newer group of Latino leaders recognize the importance of representation but seemingly not at the expense of certain ideological affinities. Among the newer generation of leaders are State Senators Jessica Ramos, Gustavo Rivera, Julia Salazar, and recently-elected Kristen Gonzalez, who would all have had a vote in LaSalle's nomination had it passed committee. Ramos and Luis Sepulveda were the two Latino senators on the Senate judiciary committee; Ramos voted against LaSalle; Sepulveda was a staunch supporter.

The current divide among Latinos immersed in political affairs in New York is clearly largely ideological. It is yet another obstacle to Latino progress, empowerment, and representation. Latinos have seemingly always had difficulties maintaining the necessary level of unity for more progress to ensue. This was the case even when Puerto Ricans were the dominant Latino group in the city. One can think of the Herman Badillo versus Ramon Velez battles, and other intra-Puerto Rican squabbles that hindered the Puerto Rican quest for fairness and representation.

Yet as Latino groups increased in numbers over the years, among them our Dominican and Mexican sisters and brothers, the rifts that some predicted never fully materialized. There has been genuine support for leaders who trace their origins to places other than Puerto Rico. For example, Puerto Rican Congresswoman Nydia Velazquez's early support of Antonio Reynoso, a Dominican who represented a City Council district (and is now Brooklyn Borough President) that had an overwhelming number of Puerto Rican voters. Then there's her support of Carlos Menchaca, a Mexican who represented a district with a large number (though now decreasing) of Puerto Ricans. Notably, Velazquez has been another prominent progressive Latina in support of Justice LaSalle.

There is also former Assemblyman Jose Rivera, who was one of the pioneering Puerto Rican political leaders who supported a number of Dominican candidates at a time when Dominicans were just beginning to increase in large numbers in the Bronx. Rivera's support for now-Assemblymember Yudelka Tapia when she ran for school board (when New York City had school boards) and his support for Nelson Castro's bid for State Assembly are indications of this.

Of course, there were and are exceptions to the work of these extraordinary leaders. But the rifts in their time were not overly detrimental to the Latino cause, even if more advancement would have been possible through more unity.

There is no obvious remedy to bridge the ideological divide that has engulfed Latino politics in New York. What does appear certain is that Latinos will continue to impede their own progress, and in consequence, make the job even easier for those who are already resisting their empowerment and advancement.

28

Illusions and Reality in New York Politics
More on Hector LaSalle's Rejection

REINHOLD NIEBUHR, ONE OF the great political theologians of the twentieth century and a co-founder of the once influential Liberal Party of New York, used to castigate the US for considering itself to be morally innocent in the world. And no wonder, given that the expansion-minded US was responsible for horrendous evils like the annihilation of indigenous and Mexican peoples. He also vituperated the country for its hypocritical foreign policy stances: it claimed that its moral superiority drove its (frankly egotistical) mission to spread its "values" globally.

This posture of innocence Niebuhr said was intended simply to disguise the covetous desires of the US.

The United States' illusions of innocence are not limited to its role in global power politics. State Senator Michael Gianaris's recent opinion piece about Hector LaSalle's nomination and eventual rejection shows that they pervade our NY state politics too. The first illusion is that the LaSalle ordeal was not one based on ideological differences; rather, it was one that reflects the dynamics "between outsiders and insiders, between reformers and the establishment."[1] For Gianaris, this is a sign that the old machinations of Albany are over.

---

1. https://www.cityandstateny.com/opinion/2023/01/opinion-lasalles-rejection-was-defeat-albany-backroom-politics/382061/

They are not. The reality is that power politics (and the LaSalle nomination process is fundamentally a matter of power politics) is riddled with the angling and backbiting which the purveyors of such politics deem necessary to obtain the results they want. Some people disguise this reality under the label "reform." Yet, the addition of four members of the state senate's judiciary committee (three of which had publicly declared themselves to be against LaSalle) unveils the illusionary mask of reform and idealism that Gianaris seems to be wearing. The lack of expert witnesses to testify at a momentous hearing to nominate the chief justice of the highest court in the state unveils this mask of illusion.

The illusion of "reform" masked the truth of the power play that led to the rejection of the first Puerto Rican Latino nominated to become the chief justice of the Court of Appeals. That power play included "packing" the committee, refusing to allow the testimony of expert witnesses (pro and con), and even perhaps the refusal to allow the nomination to reach the senate floor.

Because I am trained as a religious scholar, one deeply steeped in the progressive tradition of liberation theology, I cannot help but apply a "hermeneutics of suspicion" to the words of Senator Gianaris, and wonder if there is more going on here than a game pitting an outsider against an insider/reformer and against the establishment.

In general, the senate judiciary process has tended to be a noncontroversial affair. Nominees are rarely subjected to overly intense proceedings. However, in the case of Puerto Rican nominees, it seems that a different standard is applied. Take the case of the current Court of Appeals judge, Jenny Rivera. Though her nomination did indeed reach the full body and was confirmed by the Senate, according to The Buffalo News[2], "In a rare moment for a gubernatorial nominee to the high court, Rivera came under sharp questioning for nearly five hours by Republicans on the Senate Judiciary Committee."

Republican Senators, like former Senator John Bonacic, levied accusations that sounded awfully familiar to some that were spewed by a number of Democratic senators who grilled LaSalle in his own nomination proceedings. Said Bonacic, "I have concerns . . . that she will be prone to judicial activism . . ." Driven by my hermeneutics of suspicion, I have already said[3] that the LaSalle nomination "is yet another example of how Latinos

2. https://courts367.rssing.com/chan-6030509/all_p32.html

3. https://www.gothamgazette.com/130-opinion/11791-hector-lasalle-rejection-latinos-new-york

continuously get shafted. We can no longer say such dismissal is the fault of conservatives rather than progressives: lack of advancement for Latinos has truly become a nonpartisan affair. The shafting is equal opportunity, with Latinos consistently on the receiving end."

All this brings me back to Reinhold Niebuhr's words: there is nothing ideal about a liberal illusion that assumes innocence in a political project, particularly when the project so clearly seems to be tainted by a double standard toward a Puerto Rican Latino candidate. The danger of illusions is that they deceive—like the common liberal fancy that race(ism) does not permeate so-called progressive political work. Often work that is supposedly on behalf of the dispossessed simply whitewashes racism.

You may be thinking, "Surely *some* Latinos were against LaSalle's nomination." Here, I think of James Cone, the founder of the Black liberation theology movement and my academic advisor in graduate school. Cone suggested that liberals often use people of color as pawns to fit their agendas. Such liberals' belief that they stand on the right side of history disguises and ignores their inherent biases. And when some people of color join these causes believing in the political philosophies postulated by these liberals, they get played.

The LaSalle ordeal presents a challenging moment for the future of Latino politics in New York. No matter where we stand on the ideological spectrum, we must be willing to expose any political agenda that limits Latinos in New York rather than empowering them.

29

New York Latino Politics
Beyond New York City

On Thursday February 16, the New Rochelle City Democratic Committee made history by endorsing the mayoral candidacy of Yadira Ramos-Herbert in this year's election. An Afro-Latina of Puerto Rican and Dominican descent and currently a City Council member, Ramos-Herbert is the first person of color to receive a major party's endorsement for mayor in New York's seventh largest city. Ramos-Herbert's candidacy and the committee's endorsement helpfully remind us that Latino politics in New York is about more than New York City; the Latino presence has been and continues to be felt throughout the Empire State.

Truth be told, my columns for Gotham Gazette[1] have focused exclusively on the Latino political reality in New York City or at the statewide level. That's for one key reason: because the overwhelming majority of the Latino population in New York resides in New York City—about 67%. Most Latino elected officials in New York represent parts of Gotham as well. Yet, that focus of mine (and sometimes others') overlooks a good portion of our peoples' political realities in other parts of the state—realities that point to growing Latino communities and their significant political achievements. It is high time I correct that oversight.

1. https://www.gothamgazette.com/component/contact/contact/1492-eli
-valentin?Itemid=327

The achievements of Latinos in New Rochelle are one such example. In many ways, New Rochelle has been a city of firsts in New York. It is there where the first Mexican-born candidate was elected in New York—Roberto Lopez, elected to New Rochelle's City Council in 2007. Along with Ramos-Herbert, the current New Rochelle City Council also includes Latina Martha Lopez.

The Latino population in New Rochelle has increased rapidly over the last few decades and Latinos now comprise a third of the population in that city. Most of those Latinos are of Mexican descent. The rise of Latinos in the overall population has also resulted in an increase in the number of Latino registered voters, who have now surpassed African Americans as the largest non-white ethnic group among registered voters, forming 20% of the overall electorate. Surely Ramos-Herbert as the mayoral pick for the New Rochelle Democratic Party reflects that the future of the city is Latino.

Yet New Rochelle is not the only city in Westchester County with a growing Latino population. The city of Yonkers, the county's most populous, has the largest number of Latinos, according to census data, with 89,605 Latinos, a whopping 42% of its entire population. However, when it comes to the voting population, Latinos make up only 31% of the electorate. The city of Yonkers has one Latina in the City Council out of six council members, Corazon Pineda-Isaac, who has just declared her candidacy for mayor in this year's election. Yonkers also has a Latino representative in Westchester County's Board of Legislators—José Alvarado, who became the first Honduran to win election to a position in New York in 1982.

The Latino presence there led to the creation of the organization Hispanic Democrats of Westchester. Founded and still led by Robin Bikkal, the group has endorsed a slew of candidates up and down the county, including again supporting the candidacy of Luis Marino, who in 2021 became the first ever Latino mayor of the Village of Port Chester.

But another county not far outside of New York City has more Latinos even than Westchester—Suffolk County on Long Island. With over 332,000 people, Suffolk's Latinos make up 22% of the overall county population, but only 11% of the voting population. Its legislature has two Latinos out of 18 total seats—Sam Gonzalez and Manuel Esteban. This represents just 11% of that legislative body. Suffolk County also sent the first Long Island Latino to the State Legislature: since 2002, Assembly Member Phil Ramos has represented Central Islip in the Assembly, and is now that body's deputy speaker. Suffolk has also sent to the State Senate Monica Martinez, a Latina who previously served in Suffolk's legislature. Her brother, Antonio Martinez, is a Councilman in the town of Babylon.

Next door, Nassau is the county with the third largest Latino population outside of New York City. Latinos now make up 18% of the overall population and 11% of the voting population. And yet the Nassau County legislature currently has no Latino representation.

Further north, the cities of Buffalo and Rochester also have a Latino presence. Buffalo currently has a Latino representative in the State Assembly with Jonathan Rivera, and David Rivera is the majority leader of Buffalo's Common Council. Rochester's City Council president is Latino, Miguel Melendez. Joining him on the Council is another Latino, José Peo.

According to the National Association of Latino Elected and Appointed Officials' last published data[2] on New York's Latino political representation, there are 157 elected and appointed Latino officials in New York, outside of those elected to Congress and the State Legislature.

In short, Latino presence in political leadership is increasingly felt all over the Empire State. Yadira Ramos-Herbert's candidacy for mayor of New Rochelle is only the latest example of Latinos rising toward higher office.

2. https://naleo.org/wp-content/uploads/2022/01/2021-National-Directory-Latino-Elected-Officials.pdf

30

A Closer Look at 2022 Gubernatorial Election Results Shows Why New York Democrats Must Pay Better Attention to Latino Voters

How several hundred Latino-majority election districts voted in the 2022 gubernatorial race between Democratic Governor Kathy Hochul and Republican Congressional Representative Lee Zeldin should prompt Democrats to pay more attention to Latino voters' needs.

Perhaps the biggest finding is that Latinos—traditionally among the most loyal Democrats in the state—moved toward the Republican candidate. Though the movement *is not large enough* for Democrats to be alarmed, unless Democrats engage and invest resources in Latinos now, they can potentially see a much larger defection among Latinos.

Key findings of my new analysis of voter data by election district include:

- Turnout in 2022 increased by over 200,000 votes statewide compared to the previous gubernatorial general election in 2018, when Democratic Governor Andrew Cuomo fended off Republican County Executive Marc Molinaro's challenge.

- Despite this statewide increase, New York City saw a 15% decline in voting participation (from over 2 million voters to just under 1.8 million). By contrast, many counties outside the city, like Nassau, Suffolk, and Erie, saw increases in voting participation compared to the previous gubernatorial election. The largest increase was seen in Erie, Governor Hochul's home county.

- Statewide, Latino voting participation declined 19% from 2018 to 2022, with just under half-a-million Latinos going to the polls in 2022 (Estimates are based on my analysis of election results and the use of demographic modeling data.)

- The largest decline in Latino voting participation across overall was in New York City. Only 285,176 Latino voters cast a ballot, a 28% decline from 2018.

- Of the 285,000+ Latino voters who voted in New York City in 2022, 50% were registered Democrats compared to almost 60% in 2018, an almost 10% decline in voting participation among Latino Democrats in the city.

- Latino support in New York City for the top of the Democratic ticket declined by over 10% from 2018 to 2022. In majority Latino election districts across the city in 2018, support for Cuomo was 90–95%. Support for Molinaro registered below 5% in most of those districts. In 2022, support for Hochul in the same areas hovered between 78% and 82%. Roughly 20% of Latinos in these areas supported Zeldin.

What can we conclude from all this?

Latinos continue to support Democrats in large though decreasing numbers.

From 2018 to 2022 there was a significant decline in Latino voting participation in New York City, and an increase in Latino support for the Republican candidate for governor.

Yet that increase hardly signals a game-changing political shift in New York. We will need to wait until the 2024 election cycle for more clues about Latino voters' participation and their party preference. We may see some indications via the 2023 New York City Council elections and public polling ahead of the real evidence in the 2024 elections.

So what factors prompt both a decline in voting participation and seemingly increased support for Republicans?

While the reasons behind this decline are complex, we do know that low voter turnout among Latinos is in part a direct result of lack of investment in and engagement of Latino voters.

Bernard Fraga, in his excellent data-driven book, *The Turnout Gap*, has observed that when political parties and candidates fail to engage Latinos, turnout lags. But intentional and strategic engagement efforts, tackling critical policy issues that affect Latino communities, and investing in the political empowerment of Latinos through the support and training of Latino candidates all remind Latinos of their value and importance in the political/electoral sphere.

Factors that led to a 28% decline in Latino voting participation in New York City include the Hochul campaign and the State Democratic Party relying on surrogates and TV and radio ads. This tactic does not work for Latinos, who respond better to personal contact and sustained engagement. In short, it is the bread-and-butter grassroots approach to campaigning that Latinos respond to more favorably, and which Hochul and the state party failed to do. Furthermore, a six-figure sum was a paltry investment in the State Democratic Party's *Nueva York Initiative*—purportedly an effort to woo Latinos to the party of which Hochul is the *de facto* leader.

Back just before the 2022 general election, I warned,[1] "She may win [Latinos'] vote, but it'll likely be with a smaller margin than that of any of her Democratic predecessors." This is exactly what transpired.

The shifts we are seeing in Latino voter preference are not significant enough to conclude that Latinos are on the verge of initiating a Republican wave, though some of the shifts could make the difference in select local races like for the State Legislature or City Council. But something is happening and our leaders need to pay attention.

Many Latinos feel that Democrats are abandoning them on issues like jobs, public safety, education, and affordable housing, and in terms of their presence in our communities. In the 2024 election cycle, will we see widespread Latino defection from the Democratic Party? Or will we finally see political parties make a real investment in Latinos?

1. https://www.gothamgazette.com/130-opinion/11644-latinos-hochul-2022-election-new-york-governor

31

Is the Future Now for Latinos in New York Politics?

THE RECENT CELEBRATION OF Hispanic Heritage Month was a most appropriate time to remember the contributions of Latinos to New York politics. Once spoken of as a sleeping giant, today Latinos make up almost 30 percent of all city residents, and are the largest ethnic voting group in Gotham, constituting almost a quarter of all registered voters. In terms of raw numbers, we could easily say that the sleeping giant has awakened.

While Latinos are still underrepresented at various levels of state and city governments, we are now witnessing a new generation of Latino political representatives, many of whom have arrived in the halls of government with great potential and ambition. A few of them have even been mentioned as potential opponents to the current mayor in the 2025 municipal elections. Indeed, of the four most frequently mentioned potential challengers, three are Latino.

First, we have the current Brooklyn Borough President, Antonio Reynoso. Before his tenure in Brooklyn Borough Hall, Reynoso served two terms as a city councilman, and began his work in politics as an organizer for the now-defunct organization, ACORN. Reynoso has long been a darling of the progressive Left movement in New York, as evidenced by progressive leaders' recent meeting to discuss the possibilities of endorsing a candidate to challenge Mayor Eric Adams. Not only was Reynoso mentioned as a possible candidate, he was the only elected official present at the gathering in an unlikely locale for such discussions—Staten Island.

Though the powers of the borough presidency have dwindled significantly, the perch has proved to be a stepping for higher office. Such was the case for Scott Stringer, who was elected city comptroller in 2013 after serving as Manhattan Borough President for eight years. And of course, for eight years, our current mayor also occupied the very seat Reynoso does now.

While the position can serve as a bully pulpit to champion issues that are important to a vast constituency, for Reynoso the timing of running for mayor would be a bit complicated: he would have to forgo a re-election effort for his seat, since borough president races run in the same cycle as those for mayor.

The second potential challenger—State Senator Jessica Ramos—does not have to worry about losing a currently held seat. Since state legislative races are held in even numbered years, and municipal elections in odd years, Ramos has the luxury of setting her sights on Gracie Mansion without giving up her senate position. She has quite possibly received the most media attention of all the possible candidates I am mentioning, particularly in light of the migrant crisis engulfing our city.

Ramos is not only a fierce advocate for the proper care and management of city resources on behalf of migrants, she herself comes from a family that understands very well the plight of those seeking a better life in Gotham.

Ramos' parents migrated to New York from Colombia, putting down roots in a city that has seen one of their own rise to stardom in the senate and in city politics. Ramos worked in labor and now chairs the labor committee in the Senate. She is articulate and whip smart, and will certainly be considered for higher office for years to come.

Zellnor Myrie, one of Ramos' colleagues in the senate, is a third possible contender for the mayoralty. Myrie's parents arrived in New York from Costa Rica. His credentials are quite impressive: after his graduation from Brooklyn Technical High School, Myrie graduated from Fordham University and received his law degree from the prestigious Cornell Law School.

Interestingly enough, Myrie already has some history with Mayor Adams. In 2018, as a first-time candidate, Myrie took on the then-incumbent Senator Jesse Hamilton, a protégé of Adams, whom Hamilton succeeded in the Senate. Myrie defeated Hamilton rather impressively. But it is chiefly his hard work and intelligence as an advocate for election reform and ballot access that has won Myrie many supporters.

Any of these Latinos would present a potentially formidable challenge to Adams, particularly since Latinos were a pivotal voting bloc for the mayor. As I have previously mentioned, Adams received just over 50 percent of support in many Latino precincts in the Bronx, and received a plurality of the overall Latino vote. Any of these candidates—and perhaps Ramos in particular because of her long-standing work in Latino neighborhoods—could wrestle this bloc away from Adams, impeding him from replicating the same coalition that led him to victory in 2021.

Latino voters are no longer the only force with which our city's politics must reckon: so too is the new generation of Latino leaders.

32

Latoya Joyner's Open Seat and the Importance of the Latino Vote

ASSEMBLY MEMBER LATOYA JOYNER's recent resignation sent shock waves through the Bronx political establishment earlier this month. Joyner, a popular representative in her district and among many Bronx politicos, would likely have coasted to victory in this June's primary, but word is that she has opted to take a job in the private sector.

This leaves the Bronx Democratic organization with a major decision to make: endorse another African American candidate, continuing a 40-year tradition, or, perhaps, support a Latina/o candidate in a district that is majority Latino?

The Bronx Democratic organization holds much sway in who will get the Democratic nomination in a soon-to-be-called special election. Along with the Queens Democratic Party, the Bronx Democratic organization is considered to be a powerhouse apparatus precisely in moments like these, since they have almost entire control of the county committee members who vote for the nominee. The eventual nominee is almost guaranteed success in a special election, since the 77th Assembly district, which Joyner has represented since 2015, is overwhelmingly Democratic.

So, who will Bronx Democrats nominate? The decision should be a difficult one for one critical reason: identity politics. For, as much as some may disdain it, identity politics play a pivotal role in electoral politics, and this is certainly the case in this Assembly district. There are many people who, like me, believe that proper political representation should be an important, though not exclusive, marker for selecting candidates.

With this in mind, here are some facts that I suggest should be a top concern of those making decisions within the Bronx Democratic organization:

Of Democratic voters in this Assembly district, 51 percent are Latinos. Though in the majority, Latino voting participation here lags behind that of other ethnic groups. This has certainly been the case in the 77th Assembly district. But recent election cycles suggest an awakening of sorts, with more Latinos voting. Based on my data and calculations, in a Democratic primary this June Latinos may comprise 46 percent of the overall vote. African Americans (with a growing African population) may comprise 43 percent of the vote.

Another important data point is that 64 percent of likely voters (and this includes a potential Latino electorate) are female. I have no doubt that a well-funded and organized campaign by a Latina candidate can win in a Democratic primary—provided there are not multiple Latinos running for the seat.

An important wild card is whom Congressman Adriano Espaillat will endorse. While he only represents a small chunk of this Assembly district in Congress (compared to Congressman Ritchie Torres), Espaillat has wide name recognition among many Latino voters in the West Bronx, many of whom are of Dominican origin.

Espaillat has not been shy about bucking the Bronx Democratic machine in portions of the Bronx he represents, as he did in the neighboring 78th Assembly district where he endorsed George Alvarez over the then long-time incumbent Jose Rivera. Alvarez won that race. Will Espaillat put his thumb on the scale?

The next week or so will provide lots of answers, but even now one thing is certain: Bronx Democrats will not be able to ignore the importance of the Latino vote in this district and the all-important matter of due political representation.

33

Latino Voters Can Play Key Role in the Outcome of New York's Most Contested Primary Race

NO MATTER YOUR POLITICS, you'll probably agree that the NY-16 congressional primary, pitting the incumbent Congressman Jamaal Bowman against Westchester County Executive George Latimer, will be the most contested congressional primary battle this coming June.

The race thus far has been driven largely by the Israel-Gaza crisis. Bowman has been a staunch advocate of the Palestinian cause, decrying Israel's response to the awful Hamas attack on Oct. 7. Those defending Israel have railed against Bowman, and the American Israel Public Affairs Committee (AIPAC), the largest pro-Israel lobby group, has already poured millions into the race to support Latimer's run.

Yet while the Israel-Palestine crisis will surely be the issue that garners the most attention in this hotly contested race, Latinos could be the swing vote, contends long-time Latino commentator Howard Jordan. A close inspection of voter data, past election results, and current electoral dynamics suggest he's right.

The 16th congressional district, covering parts of Westchester and the Bronx, has over 313,000 Democratic voters. The eventual winner of the Democratic primary will be the presumptive winner in November, since the district is heavily Democratic and thus is not in play for Republicans. Of these voters, 21 percent are Latino, 42 percent of whom live in the city of Yonkers. The bulk of the rest of Latinos in this district are in Westchester County, residing in cities like New Rochelle, Mount Vernon, and White Plains, with 13 percent in the Bronx portion.

The familiar growth of Latino communities in various sections of New York is certainly true in this mostly suburban district. While Yonkers has long had a large and mostly Puerto Rican voting population, other suburban cities in the district, like New Rochelle and Mount Vernon, have experienced significant Latino population growth over the last couple of decades. New Rochelle also recently elected the first Afro-Latino mayor in its history.

All these numbers highlight the critical role that Latino voters will play in determining the outcome of the primary. There is no doubt that, should Latimer or Bowman ignore this important base, it would be at their own peril. Interestingly, both candidates have previously represented these areas, Bowman in Congress and Latimer as Westchester County Executive.

As a political observer and analyst but also as a voter in this district, I note that thus far both candidates have failed to engage Latino voters adequately. Initial mailers (and there have been plenty between the candidates and the respective PACs weighing in on the race) did not articulate their messages in both Spanish and English, and it has not been Latinos who have been out canvassing, or reaching Latino voters in their homes. Latimer's campaign, however, has recently been more intentional about utilizing bilingual messaging.

It is clear through a number of recent public polls that Latinos are mainly concerned about economic matters—specifically, the cost of living, adequate wages, and affordable housing. Bowman's progressive stance and advocacy for marginalized communities may resonate with many Latino voters who seek representation that understands their struggles and aspirations. On the other hand, Latimer's extensive experience in local government and his focus on practical solutions may appeal to Latino voters looking for stability and tangible results.

As Election Day approaches, both campaigns would do well to intensify their outreach efforts, focusing on the issues that matter most to Latino communities, and communicating this message in a culturally sensitive and intentional way. The candidate who successfully addresses these concerns and builds a strong rapport with Latino voters will have an added advantage come Tuesday night.

34

Latinos in New York and the 2024 Presidential Election

"LATINO VOTERS ARE DEFECTING to the Republican Party." "Latinos cost Kamala Harris the presidency." Since election night, Latinos seem to have become the scapegoat for Democrats' loss of the White House. Then there are the claims like, "Trump wins a bigger share of the Latino vote in New York City."

Is that last claim true? Well, yes. But it is unhelpful to define Latinos as one big, broad group as it is complicated to explain Trump's apparent increase in the Latino vote.

To make sense of the blaming and claiming, I have analyzed precinct-by-precinct (or in New York terminology, election districts) the presidential election results in the Bronx, Brooklyn, Manhattan, and Queens. Though Staten Island has a growing Latino voting population, its density is not sufficient to include here.

My data comes from the now official election results provided by the New York City Board of Elections. I modeled the Latino demographics using L2's voter database (L2 is a nonpartisan voter data company utilized by many campaigns, academics and some major media outlets), election results, demographic modeling of the voter file, and looking at specific Latino-heavy neighborhoods, while factoring in the changes of election districts that occur every ten years as a result of redistricting efforts.

Based on this preliminary analysis, I learned that: Trump's share of Latino support across these four boroughs did indeed increase, with the largest increase coming from Latinos in Queens. However, Latinos still give the Democratic nominee the majority of their vote. Contrary to what we have seen in some parts of the country, there is no indication of Latinos defecting en masse from voting for Democrats to choosing Republicans (like in Passaic and Hudson counties across the river in New Jersey). I characterize the 2024 shift not so much as a defection as a repudiation of the Biden administration's policy positions, years of neglect of the Latino plight, and political parties' lack of real engagement with Latino voters. In New York, the majority of Latinos are registered Democrats. Thus, we must ask: why has the state Democratic party failed to engage this constituency despite its loyalty to the Democratic cause?

Taking a look at each of the four boroughs, we can note the following:

The largest concentration of Latinos in Manhattan is in the Washington Heights area, almost all of it within the 72nd Assembly district. As in the districts I have examined, I have lasered in on precincts that are at least 50% Latino, which in this district is the majority of the entire Assembly district. In 2024, Trump appears to have won 31% support from Latino voters, a 14% increase over his 2020 margin.

Naturally, Trump's increase represents a decrease for the presidential Democratic nominee, Kamala Harris. Whereas Biden received 83% of the Latino vote there, Harris received only 69%.

Within the 68th Assembly district, which mostly covers East Harlem and contains the second largest Latino concentration in Manhattan, though Harris's numbers were better than in the 72nd Assembly district, they were 9% less than Biden in 2020. Overall, I estimate Harris received about 75% of the vote in Latino-majority election districts across Manhattan.

Moving north to the Bronx presents us with some fascinating findings, with some differences in levels of support for Harris across Assembly districts. In the 78th Assembly district, for instance, Latino support for Harris was 15% less than for Biden in 2000 with only 69% of this Latino-majority district. The South Bronx 84th Assembly district did not see such a drastic shift, decreasing from 77% support for Biden to 74% for Harris.

Other Latino-majority Assembly districts in the Bronx, like the 85th and 86th Assembly districts, saw 9 to 12% decreases for the Democratic presidential candidate. Thus, in the only Latino-majority borough in the

City of New York, despite strong Latino support for the Democratic presidential candidate, a decline is evident.

A move east to Queens shows a particularly strong decline in Latino support for Harris compared to Biden in 2020, indeed a greater decline than any other district with a large Latino presence.

In Latino-majority election districts in Assembly districts 34, 35, and 39 (the neighborhoods of Corona, Elmhurst and East Elmhurst), I found:

Between the three I note an 18% decline in support for Democrats (Harris compared to Biden).

Past levels of support for Democratic candidates from Latinos were similar across the boroughs. Why the difference now? Perhaps it is due to the growing discontent within Latino communities in Queens, stemming largely from frustrations over public safety and quality-of-life issues that many people have attributed to an out-of-control migrant crisis. As detailed in a recent New York Magazine article, shifts in voter sentiment among Latinos are partly influenced by their experiences with local policies, public safety concerns, and perceptions of the current administration's handling of key issues.

Results in Brooklyn appear to be similar to those of Latinos in The Bronx and Manhattan. Taking a look at the 51st Assembly district, which covers Latino-heavy Sunset Park, Harris earned 57% of the vote in Latino-majority election districts, a 14% decrease from Biden's results in 2020. Results in the 53rd Assembly district (representing portions of Latinos in Bushwick) and the 54th Assembly district (parts of East New York) show Harris hovering around the 70% mark, about a 5% decline from four years before.

There are some stark differences in voting preference between the 51st Assembly district and the 53rd and 54th Assembly districts of Brooklyn. The 51st district is home to a large number of Latinos who arrived from other countries after the longer presence of Puerto Ricans in New York. Are more recent Latino arrivals more concerned and aggravated by the arrival of newer Latino groups than are their Puerto Rican counterparts? The state board of elections voter file updates will give us a more detailed picture of what transpired, but for now we must ask the question since these differences in Latino voting patterns are rising.

Any discussion about changes in voting preferences must take into account voter registration patterns, since they can provide other clues about any potential "defections." I examined two sets of voter registration periods—the one leading into the 2020 presidential election and the other leading into the 2024 presidential election. My analysis for the former begins in 2018, the year of the midterm election; my analysis of the latter begins in 2022, which marks the most recent midterm. Here is what I have discovered:

From 2022 to 2024 I note a steep decline in new Latino registrants compared to the 2018 to 2020 period. Only 87,252 Latinos registered to vote during this time period (compared to 201,878 in the previous period). Of these, 43% registered as Democrats, 42% as nonaffiliated, and 12% as Republicans. Not only do we observe a 57% decline in new Latino registrants, we also note a decline in those registering with the Democratic Party. And it is perhaps this dynamic that may say more about the future of Latino voting realities than one presidential election cycle. Through these registration numbers and the numerous public polls that have come out over the last few years, it is clear that Latinos are largely discontent with the current political and social realities; no wonder: Latinos bear the brunt of social, economic and political calamities. My fear is that instead of using these realities as motivational tools or means to express their desires at the ballot box, Latinos may be choosing not to participate in the political process at all.

Since the 2018 election cycle, Latino voting participation in New York has declined significantly, no doubt for many different reasons. Whether by voting preferences or lack of political participation, Latinos are clearly expressing their discontent. Are our political leaders and parties paying attention? Given Latinos' numbers and plight, I surely hope so.

35

A New Rumble in the Bronx
Battle for the Borough Presidency

WITH ALL EYES ON the race for the mayoralty, fewer New York City voters have yet glanced north to the Bronx, where a rumble of its own is shaping up. Rafael Salamanca, currently a councilman and chair of the Council's powerful Land Use Committee, is challenging the incumbent borough president, Vanessa Gibson. Several dynamics make this a race worth watching.

Having won office four years ago, Gibson has one term left. Taking on an incumbent, who in this case is fairly well liked across the Bronx, does not happen often. But Salamanca has made the bold move, and might actually give Gibson a run for her money.

As a councilman with years of experience under his belt, Salamanca is no ordinary insurgent. Not only does he bring to the race the claim of city legislative experience (which Gibson has as well, from her previous Council experience and her current borough presidential role), he also comes to the race having raised a whopping $653,987, double the amount the incumbent Gibson has. At least in terms of fundraising, Salamanca clearly has not been hampered by the typical insurgent woes.

Gibson has received over $184,557 more than Salamanca in public matching money. Yet Salamanca's massive fundraising haul in private donations, and a lower spend up to this point in the campaign, has left him with a $300,000-plus spending advantage heading into the last six weeks of the race. At least when it comes to money, Salamanca has an edge.

But money isn't everything, at least not in this race. Salamanca is taking on a well-liked incumbent in Gibson. She has the backing of the Bronx Democratic Party, the powerful union 1199, the Working Families Party, and numerous elected officials (many of whom are Latino) across the Bronx. For most insurgents, taking on an incumbent with this level of support usually spells trouble. Can Salamanca defy the odds?

He has certainly removed the usual fundraising advantage that most incumbents enjoy. But what about other factors? Does Salamanca have a path given that the Bronx is the only Latino-majority borough? According to the most recent voter file, Latinos comprise 46 percent of all registered Bronx Democrats. The next largest group, based on excellent data from the firm L2, is Black voters at 35 percent.

This may seem to suggest an advantage for Salamanca. However, things are a bit more complicated in the Bronx for anyone considering the Latino vote as an exclusive path to victory (this is not to say that this is Salamanca's strategy). For one, the Latino vote alone is not enough to give any candidate the win. Moreover, Latino voting participation in the Bronx, as in other places, lags behind other groups.

Let's take a look at numbers from the last municipal election in the Bronx in 2021, when Gibson was first elected as borough president.

Several elements are important to understand here. First, only 20 percent of eligible Bronx voters came out to the polls in the 2021 election. In Manhattan, 34 percent of eligible voters went to the polls. In Brooklyn, it was 29 percent. Similar rates applied in Queens and Staten Island. The Bronx is the borough with the lowest voting participation rates in the city— for reasons I won't address here.

Moreover, not only is voting participation low borough-wide, it's particularly low among Latinos. Only 15 percent of eligible Latino Democratic voters participated in the 2021 election. By comparison, 24 percent of eligible Black voters went to the polls, as did 29 percent of (the considerably fewer) eligible white voters.

When it comes to Latino voting participation the question remains: What is holding Latinos back from participating in elections? Unfortunately, many Latino elected officials in the borough are neglecting to engage the question.

All this notwithstanding, Salamanca will need to win the lion's share of the Latino vote to make this a competitive race. If Gibson manages to pull enough Latinos to her column, which is not impossible for her to do, Salamanca will have a very long night on election day.

If this race comes down to voters making choices by fealty to race and ethnicity, my eyes will be glued to results in neighborhoods that are mostly non-Black and Latino. Almost half of these voters are in Riverdale, where a key Gibson supporter, Assemblyman Jeffrey Dinowitz, has his base.

Another 21 percent of these voters reside in Morris Park, City Island, and Pelham Bay, areas represented by another Gibson backer, Assemblyman Michael Benedetto. Both Dinowitz and Benedetto have long been party stalwarts, and their support for Gibson will be critical in this race. In addition to pulling out the Latino vote, Salamanca's chances will depend on how many of these voters he'll be able to convince.

Clearly much is at stake for both candidates. Gibson is the only incumbent borough president facing a serious challenge. And Salamanca aspires to be the fifth Latino borough president of the Condado de la Salsa. One thing is for sure: with fewer than six weeks to go, this rumble in the Bronx will become more contentious before it is over.

36

Latino Vote 2025
City Council Races to Watch

WITH ALL EYES SEEMINGLY glued to the New York City mayoral race, many voters are paying less attention to a number of competitive Council races across the city. A new Council composition will surely have implications for who will be the legislative body's next speaker, and for the purposes of this article and series, there will be potential ramifications for Latino representation as well.

This column looks at seven Council races in this month's primary, spanning three boroughs—Manhattan, the Bronx and Queens. These districts are either Latino plurality or majority districts, with two districts that are not overwhelmingly Latino in population but have Latino elected representation.

MANHATTAN'S DISTRICT 1 (FINANCIAL DISTRICT, LOWER EAST SIDE, SOHO, TRIBECA)

Incumbent Christopher Marte, a one-term councilmember of Dominican heritage, is locked in a fierce battle against several challengers—Jess Coleman, Elizabeth Lewinsohn, and Eric Yu. Typically incumbents do not mind going up against multiple challengers at once. The conventional wisdom is that having more than one opponent often leads to a split in the anti-incumbent vote, giving an edge to the person already holding the seat.

This time, however, Marte faces a real challenge, for two of his opponents are well funded. Coleman has received the maximum allowed in public financing—$192,543—and has raised $61,710 in private, individual contributions. This has given him a $254,244 campaign kitty, a formidable amount for an insurgent.

Lewinsohn has opted out of the New York City public financing program and has depended solely on private, individual contributions. She has been able to raise a whopping $664,877—an astronomical amount of money in a Council race, especially coming from an insurgent. Just as incredible is her spending: as of the last campaign finance filing, Lewinsohn had already spent $603,255.

Marte, the incumbent, has raised a total of $279,703 of private and public monies. He not only faces one opponent who had double that amount, but has earned the scorn of some local residents who see him as an anti-development advocate at a time when affordable housing is desperately needed.

Marte, for instance, voted against the City of Yes zoning reforms. He retorts, however, that affordable housing is the major issue in his district, and that development should not come at the expense of the displacement of long-time residents who may be priced out of continued luxury housing development.

The demographic realities of this district are quite fascinating. Among the registered Democrats, 39 percent are white, a quarter are Asian, and 15 percent are Latino. There's a small Black electorate, comprising about 3 percent of the district.

Interestingly, of the seven districts written about here, Marte's is one of two represented by a Latino in a district that is neither a Latino-majority nor a Latino-plurality. Considering likely voting participation, white residents represent 44 percent of the district, Asian residents 24 percent, and Latinos 10 percent. The current dynamics in this race surely makes this a toss-up.

MANHATTAN'S DISTRICT 2 (GREENWICH VILLAGE, LOWER EAST SIDE, EAST VILLAGE, MIDTOWN SOUTH-FLATIRON-UNION SQUARE, GRAMERCY, MURRAY HILL-KIPS BAY)

This race is a particularly interesting one. It is an open seat, as Carlina Rivera, the current councilmember, is term limited. The race is between

Harvey Epstein, a current Assemblyman, local community activist Andrea
Gordillo, Allie Ryan, Sarah Batchu, and finally Anthony Weiner, the dis-
graced congressman and former mayoral candidate.

In all likelihood, the results of the race will spell the end of over 30
years of Puerto Rican representation in this district. Back in 1991, Antonio
Pagan defeated the then long-time incumbent, Miriam Friedlander, in a
squeaker of a race. His win was a victory for a Puerto Rican community
that had long sought political representation.

The Lower East Side, one of the neighborhoods in this district, had for
years been a locus of thriving Puerto Rican activism, and cultural pride has
been palpable in the streets, meeting halls, poet dens like the Nuyorican
Poets Cafe, and even local churches. It was the artistic birthplace of the
spoken word poets Pedro Pietri and Miguel Piñero, and also the place
where women like Margarita Lopez developed into fierce advocates of the
advancement of Puerto Rican people. In fact, Lopez succeeded Pagan in the
Council in 1997.

Behind Lopez was Rosie Mendez, and then Carlina Rivera replaced
the term-limited Mendez. In short, three Puerto Rican women succeeded
each other and together represented a Council district for almost three decades. No other district represented by a Latina/o—whether for a Council,
Congress, or a state legislative seat—has been able to replicate this remark-
able feat.

After next week, this rich history of Puerto Rican representation will
come to an end in this district. No Puerto Rican is on the ballot; Andrea
Gordillo is of Peruvian descent.

To add further credence to the likely end of Puerto Rican-Latino
representation, one must look at the demographic realities of the district.
The Democratic electorate is almost half white, followed by Latinos at 19
percent. Asian voters come in third with 10 percent. Black voters comprise
4 percent of all Democratic voters here.

Taking into account likely voting participation, 55 percent of the likely
voters in this district will be white. The next closest ethnic group are likely
to be Latinos, at 12 percent. Epstein would seem to have an advantage in
this race, having represented much of the area in the Assembly, and having
earned the support of many local leaders over the years.

MANHATTAN AND THE BRONX, DISTRICT 8 (MOTT HAVEN-PORT MORRIS, MELROSE, CONCOURSE-CONCOURSE VILLAGE, UPPER EAST SIDE-CARNEGIE HILL, UPPER EAST SIDE-YORKVILLE, EAST HARLEM)

Moving up north in the island of Manhattan is District 8, which covers a small portion of Upper Yorkville, most of East Harlem, and parts of the South Bronx. The district is a majority-Latino district, mostly people of Puerto Rican descent. Besides District 2, District 8 has the potential to become the only other district to be represented by three consecutive Puerto Rican women.

Starting the trend was Melissa Mark-Viverito in 2005. Mark-Viverito eventually became the first Latina speaker of the City Council. Diana Ayala replaced her because of term limits, and now Ayala will leave after serving her two terms.

Both Mark-Viverito and Ayala have endorsed Elsie Encarnacion, a Puerto Rican woman and Ayala's chief of staff. But Encarnacion faces strong opponents. She's one of seven candidates who have earned a spot on the ballot. Among the competitors are Clarisa Alayeto (of Cuban descent), Federico Colon, Rosa Diaz, Wilfredo Lopez, Nicholas Reyes, and finally Raymond Santana, one of the Central Park Five.

The race seems to be coming down to a three-person contest—Encarnacion, Lopez, and Alayeto. It has also earned the attention and financial resources of a number of outside groups that have contributed hundreds of thousands of dollars in independent expenditures. I will say more about this later. For now, suffice it to note that Encarnacion and Lopez have been the beneficiaries of this spending. The race promises to be one of the hottest Council primaries to watch.

THE BRONX'S DISTRICT 13 (BRUCKNER, THROGGS NECK, PELHAM BAY, CITY ISLAND, FERRY POINT PARK, PELHAM PARKWAY-VAN NEST, MORRIS PARK) AND DISTRICT 14 (UNIVERSITY HEIGHTS, MOUNT HOPE, FORDHAM HEIGHTS, BEDFORD PARK, KINGSBRIDGE HEIGHTS-VAN CORTLANDT VILLAGE, KINGSBRIDGE-MARBLE HILL)

The most northern New York City borough, The Bronx, has two races that are holding my attention, in Districts 13 and 14.

In District 13, six candidates are vying for the seat now occupied by the Republican Kristy Marmorato, who defeated the first Latina ever to represent this district—Marjorie Velazquez. Democratic primary voters will choose among the following candidates: Shirley Aldebol, David Diaz, John Perez, Joel Rivera, and Theona Reets-Dupont.

This race seems to be coming down to Shirley Aldebol and Joel Rivera. Aldebol has earned the support of numerous labor organizations, having herself worked at 32BJ for two decades. And the Bronx Democratic Party has also thrown its support behind Aldebol. She has received $137,191 and, together with the private, individual contributions, has managed to bring in $185,924. With public financing and private contributions, Rivera has brought in $107,824.

Rivera is no stranger to politics. He ran for Council in a different Bronx district in 2013 and comes from a background of activism and non-profit work. His father is the well-known and highly respected bishop, Raymond Rivera. Joel Rivera will not make this easy for Aldebol and will certainly give her a run for her money.

To the west we move to District 14, and what may be the most contested Council race in the city. Incumbent Pierina Sanchez will face her predecessor, Fernando Cabrera. A third candidate, Bryan Hodge-Vasquez, is also making a go at it, and has managed to pull in $144,559 between public and private monies. However, because of name recognition and how institutional powers have weighed in, this race will likely come down to Sanchez and Cabrera.

Cabrera represented this district for 12 years. As a result of term limits, he ran for Bronx Borough President in 2021, losing to the current incumbent Vanessa Gibson. Sanchez has earned the support of the Bronx Democratic Party, a number of labor organizations, and has out-fundraised Cabrera. Among her colleagues in the Council, she is known to be a bright and talented representative. However, Cabrera is still known among many of the voters in this district, and for this reason he'll be a tough opponent to beat.

District 14 has been rocked by rising crime. An excellent Bronx Times profile of the race reminds us that major crimes have risen by 12.75 percent in the 46th police precinct, and 10.94 percent in the 52nd over the past two years. Both precincts reside in this Council district. Will voters in District 14, who are largely concerned about crime and affordability issues, castigate Sanchez at the ballot box? We shall see next week.

QUEENS' DISTRICT 21 (ASTORIA-DITMARS-STEINWAY, JACKSON HEIGHTS, EAST ELMHURST, ELMHURST, CORONA, REGO PARK, FLUSHING-WILLETS POINT) AND DISTRICT 25 (JACKSON HEIGHTS, ELMHURST, EAST ELMHURST, WOODSIDE)

District 21 is an open race as a result of Francisco Moya completing both terms. Four candidates are now vying for this seat, which covers Corona, East Elmhurst, Jackson Heights and Lefrak City: David Aiken, Yanna Henriquez, Erycka Montoya, and Shanel Thomas-Henry. Several dynamics have made this race perhaps the one to watch in Queens. First, the still influential Queens Democratic machine has backed Henriquez. Moya has also recently thrown his support behind her. (Moya has been a key Queens machine loyalist, so this support should come as no surprise.)

Interestingly, Montoya, who happens to be a staffer for the current Council Speaker and mayoral candidate Adrienne Adams, has received the support of Congresswoman Alexandria Ocasio-Cortez, Assemblymembers Catalina Cruz and Jessica Gonzalez-Rojas, the Working Families Party and numerous labor organizations.

While many of the candidates backed by the Queens' Democratic machine have been successful in many parts of the borough, this particular district and its accompanying neighborhoods have been known to back anti-machine candidates. In many ways, it was former Councilman and State Senator Hiram Monserrate who began what would become insurgents bucking machine-backed candidates. And though Monserrate ended his tenure in the Senate in disgrace, he's largely had success electing district leaders and judges running in these neighborhoods.

This race has in many ways become a proxy battle between the machine candidate versus a candidate backed by progressive organizations and elected officials that have, at times, been willing to buck the Queens' establishment. And lastly, like the race in District 8, this battle has seen a large sum of money from outside groups.

In District 25, the incumbent Shekar Krishnan faces Ricardo Pacheco, who also ran two years ago. The district is a Latino-plurality district, with Latinos representing almost 40 percent of the electorate. When factoring in likely voters, the electorate will probably be evenly split across ethnic lines, giving us another indication that Latinos continue to underperform in elections in terms of turnout. Krishnan has vastly out-raised Pacheco, and seems likely to win re-election.

THE ROLE OF INDEPENDENT EXPENDITURES

I feel obliged to insert a closing word on the role outside groups are playing in a number of these races. Ever since the Citizens United decision in 2010, we have seen an eventual proliferation of independent spending in local races in New York. In the current mayoral race, outside groups have spent over $19 million, most of that to support former Gov. Andrew Cuomo's candidacy.

These outside groups are not limiting their contributions to citywide or statewide races. They're now also spending heavily on local Council contests. In fact, four of the seven districts examined here have seen the impact of these independent expenditures. Take District 8, for example. Of the seven districts, this one has seen the most money spent for various candidates, with Elsie Encarnacion receiving the most. Almost $600,000 has been spent to boost her candidacy. Wilfredo Lopez has been the beneficiary of $453,578 spent on his behalf, while $279,475 has been spent to support Clarisa Alayeto. All told, over $1.3 million has been spent to influence voters in District 8, one of the poorest in the city.

Over $1 million has been spent in District 21, and close to half a million dollars in District 14. Does the influence of these outside groups in city races, most of which are funded by billionaires and hedge funders, undermine the purpose of the city's public matching system? The city's campaign finance law was meant to reduce the influence of big money by establishing a generous public financing program, provided that candidates agreed to abide by certain rules—like establishing contribution limits and banning corporate money.

But the new rules which have resulted from Citizens United have instead made possible a disparity between the regulations governing candidate committees and those applied to outside groups, creating an alarming imbalance. While candidate committees face stringent caps on contributions and expenditures to which I have alluded above, these outside groups operate with no such limitations. This creates an uneven playing field on which entrenched powers can perpetuate their influence unchallenged.

And as we can see from the above, the spending is not limited to affluent districts; more and more, we are seeing this influence in the poorest of districts. Perhaps the next mayor and City Council can tackle some of these issues in the coming year.

37

Latino Voters and the Political Earthquake in New York

ELECTIONS THAT PRODUCE SEISMIC shifts in the political landscape are rare. With the shocking election of Zohran Mamdani, a 33-year-old Democratic Socialist Assemblyman from Queens, New York experienced one of these shifts. Indeed, Mamdani's victory in the Democratic primary is better understood as an unexpected political earthquake.

Few expected Mamdani to win. Many observers wondered whether Mamdani could pull together the type of coalition that was needed to defeat a longtime political powerhouse. Could he expand the electorate? Could he energize younger voters? Could he appeal to and turn out low-propensity voters like Asians and Latinos? Apparently Mamdani did all the above. And interestingly, it appears that he has won a plurality of the Latino vote.

That in itself is a feat. Conventional wisdom held that Mamdani could not peel away enough Latino voters from Cuomo, considering that Latinos have always viewed Cuomo favorably. Amidst all of Cuomo's troubles, Latinos remained loyal to a governor they felt had responded to many of their needs. When Hurricane Maria ravaged the island of Puerto Rico, Cuomo stepped up by coordinating flights to deliver goods and emergency services assistance. Likewise his responses to crises in the Dominican Republic. Latinos remember such efforts.

So, what gives? How and where did Mamdani manage to win a crucial voting bloc that Cuomo needed? I have examined the preliminary first round votes of the mayoral candidates within Latino-majority election districts. These Latino-majority election districts have been identified using the L2 voter file, which provides one of the better demographic modeling data available. The New York Times has actually provided an excellent breakdown of the election results based on a number of demographic information, including ethnicity. However, its source for ethnicity information is US Census and City Planning data. My identification of Latino-majority election districts uses L2 data, which not only draws on Census information but also numerous other sources to identify ethnic information as precisely as possible. With this data, I have lasered in on election districts that are 60%+ Latino, so as to avoid the complications of deciphering Latino voters in election districts that are more diverse. (Until voter files are updated, we will not have a complete picture of the magnitude of this election. Thus, all current analyses, including this one, demand caution.)

Here's what I found:

In Manhattan, Mamdani outdid Cuomo by just over 2,000 votes. His greatest success was in Washington Heights and Inwood, the 72nd Assembly district. Mamdani lost the Latino-majority election districts in the Lower East Side by 151 votes. He won the super-majority Latino election districts in East Harlem (68th Assembly District) by 92 votes and the 71st Assembly district, covering parts of Hamilton Heights, Harlem, and lower Washington Heights by 657 votes. Remember, I am only examining super-majority Latino election districts, so these results do not refer to the overall vote in these respective districts.

Most of the elected officials in these districts notably did not endorse Mamdani, including Congressman Adriano Espaillat, whose congressional district encompasses all these neighborhoods. Only State Senator Robert Jackson and Council Member Carmen De La Rosa endorsed the presumptive Democratic nominee. (I am not factoring in those elected to party positions who made their own endorsements in the race.)

The Bronx tells a different story with the Latino vote. Cuomo handily beat Mamdani in most of the majority-Latino sections in the Bronx. Recall that the Bronx is the only majority-Latino borough in the city. In the South Bronx, 51% of voters went for Cuomo. In the Kingsbridge, Fordham, Belmont neighborhoods 51% of voters went for Cuomo and 39% for Mamdani. Of the Soundview, Longwood and Hunts Point neighborhoods,

57% of the votes went for Cuomo. Mamdani held on to 31% of the vote. And we see similar results in the Morris Heights, University Heights, and Tremont neighborhoods. In the Bronx, too, Cuomo earned the lion's share of endorsements from Latino elected officials (State Senator Gustavo Rivera bucked the trend, strongly supporting Mamdani). This election proves once again that most endorsements are meaningless and very few endorsers have the capacity to move the needle on any given election.

Moving to Brooklyn, I note that Mamdani won these super-majority Latino election districts over Cuomo by a total of 1,664 votes. Mamdani's largest support was in the Sunset Park (51st Assembly District), Bushwick, and Williamsburg neighborhoods (53rd Assembly District). Because of the stark gentrification of these neighborhoods, especially the latter two, I have been especially careful to identify those precincts which are 60%+ Latino. In the 54th Assembly District, covering parts of East New York and Cypress Hills, Mamdani bested Cuomo by 21 votes.

The Queens results in Latino neighborhoods present us with even more fascinating realities. I looked at the 60%+ Latino election districts in Corona, Elmhurst, East Elmhurst, Ozone Park and Ridgewood. Mamdani won those precincts by 1,151 votes. While these numbers may appear to be similar to results in Manhattan and Brooklyn, the reality is that these results are showing an interesting dynamic in Latino voting patterns, particularly in Queens.

My analysis[1] of the presidential election in Queens showed an increase in support for Donald Trump, though this increase was not as pronounced as some were thinking. Of all Latino neighborhoods in the city, the Queens portions showed the most significant decline in support for the Democratic presidential nominee, Kamala Harris. Recalling this very recent history makes the current mayoral primary results in these neighborhoods seem erratic. How could Latinos vote for a Democratic Socialist after voting for the conservative authoritarianism of a Donald Trump?

If anything, these results remind us yet again of what has now become almost a cliché: Latinos are not homogenous. We do not fit any once-size-fits-all type of formulations. Latinos are quite diverse in cultural variety, countries of origin, language nuances, and political philosophies. This can also be seen at the ballot box. In fact, we can see it in this election—most

1. https://www.cityandstateny.com/opinion/2024/12/commentary-latinos-new-york-and-2024-presidential-election/401837/

Bronx Latinos went with Cuomo, while a plurality of Latinos in other boroughs went with Mamdani.

Moreover, Latino support for Mamdani, particularly in Queens, should help us understand that the increase in support for Trump in 2024 was not necessarily an indication of an ideological rightward shift. What these results may be telling us is that economic populist messaging resonates deeply with Latino audiences. And this should come as no surprise. It surely was not a surprise for Mamdani. Mamdani, a truly generational political talent, has understood quite well the plight of struggling communities, like Latinos, whose quotidian realities evoke continuing economic anxieties.

A recent Columbia Center on Poverty and Social Policy and Robinhood report shows that Latinos are the poorest ethnic group in New York City, followed closely by Asians and then Blacks. It should come as no surprise, then, that Mamdani, who lasered in on affordability issues, would earn the support of a plurality of Latinos, and win the Asian vote. Mamdani's support among Blacks in the city was also higher than some anticipated.

It should also come as no surprise that most Latinos do not see fare free buses, no cost childcare, and freezing rents as a vice. These are issues that Latinos care deeply about because their very livelihoods depend on all these important day-to-day matters being affordable.

To the Democratic and Republican establishments, then, especially those gearing up for re-election next year, I would say: pay attention to the Mamdani campaign. It seems many Latinos are, and they will certainly make their opinions heard at the ballot box again.

38

What We Can Learn From the First Poll of Latino Voters in NYC's 2025 Mayoral Race

A NEW POLL IN the New York City mayoral race just landed. This is the first poll focused exclusively on New York City Latino voters in this electoral cycle, and will likely be the only one: few polls are ever taken to take the pulse of the issues important to Latino voters and the candidates they prefer. The Hispanic Federation, which commissioned this poll, must be commended for this admirable and needed work.

The findings provide some clues as to why a plurality of Latino voters supported Zohran Mamdani in the primary, and why they remain supportive as he heads into this last stretch of the campaign. My analysis of the mayoral primary in June showed that Mamdani won a plurality of support in majority-Latino election districts.

However, the nuances in voting patterns across boroughs and neighborhoods that I describe in that column point to the fact that, "Latinos are not homogeneous. We do not fit any once-size-fits-all formulations. Latinos are quite diverse in cultural variety, countries of origin, language nuances, and political philosophies." Thus we find that this variety manifests itself in particular voting patterns: for example, Queens and Manhattan Latino voters supported Mamdani in higher numbers than Latinos in the Bronx.

The Hispanic Federation (HF)-commissioned poll in many ways reflects this very dynamic, and thus mirrors what we saw in the June primary. Another excellent poll undertaken in August by Adam Carlson and Amit Singh Bagga, two of the brightest minds in politics today, found patterns identical to the HF poll and its findings about the primary results. Carlson and Singh Bagga, interviewing 200 Latinos within a wider poll to New York City voters, were able, like the HF poll, to poll Latinos by countries of origin—specifically Puerto Rican and Dominicans voters and Central and South Americans.

On the horserace question, the Carlson and Singh Bagga poll had Latino likely voters supporting Mamdani over Cuomo at 54 percent to 24 percent. I must also note that based on the dynamics at that time, the poll was a five-person race. Since then, attorney Jim Walden and Mayor Eric Adams dropped out. The HF poll includes the three-person contest—Mamdani, Andrew Cuomo and Curtis Sliwa—the race has become.

The results of the horserace question in the HF poll show Mamdani besting Cuomo 48–24, with Sliwa at a distant 14 percent. Mamdani's strong support among Latinos can be explained by a number of elements to which the poll points. The first and most important correlation seems connected to the issues most important to Latinos: cost of living, inflation, and housing costs.

Which leads me to believe that Fiorello LaGuardia's adage about municipal governing, "There is no Democratic or Republican way of cleaning the streets," may now be applied to matters relating to affordability. It is clear that there is no partisan way to speak about an affordability crisis that many Latinos are experiencing firsthand.

I say this because some quarters have sought to peg Mamdani as a radical socialist and thus as someone New York City voters should be frightened of. According to the HF poll, Mamdani is the only one in the poll who surpassed the 50 percent favorability mark. In fact, his favorability rating is at 56 percent of Latino voters polled.

Several other findings present fascinating insights. One in particular is the nuance that exists in Latino voting preference according to age and educational attainment. Mamdani's vote share with Latinos is higher among 18- to 40-year-old voters than among voters 50 and over. Differences also exist between Latinos with college degrees and those without. While 53 percent of Latinos with college degrees give Mamdani their vote, 45 percent of non-college graduates support the Democratic nominee.

Interestingly, Adam Carlson has noted a pattern in a tweet, one that connects Latinos and the rest of the electorate: "The major fault lines of this general election are not race, but rather age and educational attainment. Across racial groups, young voters and voters with a four-year college degree are way more likely to support Mamdani."

There is one last element evident from this poll (and Carlson's and Singh Bagga's) that coincides with my analysis in June's mayoral primary election. I observe some voting preference differences according to boroughs and neighborhoods, and according to Latino countries of origin.

Mamdani's strongest support among Latinos comes from voters from South American and Mexican backgrounds, followed by voters of Dominican and Puerto Rican origins. (I must note that within the voting population, Puerto Rican and Dominican voters vastly outnumber other Latino groups in the city and state. This largely coincides with the reality of the overall Latino population in the city, where Dominicans are now the largest Latino group, followed closely by Puerto Ricans, who historically were the largest Latino group in Gotham. Puerto Rican voters still remain the largest Latino voting group in the city and state.)

This explains in some ways, though not entirely, why Mamdani's support is greater in Queens, where the bulk of South American-born voters live and vote, than, say, the Bronx, where the overwhelming number of Latino voters are Puerto Rican and Dominican.

Some may be wondering: Why the difference between Puerto Rican/Dominican voters (for the purposes of this column and brevity's sake, I will refer to these voters as "Caribbean voters"), and South/Central American voters, and the difference in support among Latinos by borough?

I must acknowledge that my postulations here are, in essence, working hypotheses informed by data analysis and the historical experience of Latinos in New York. This is just one theory. I also confess humility with any speculations dealing with a broad and diverse group that has so often been captured by a singular term, whether that term is Latino, Latinx, Hispanic, or Latiné. Clearly, much more analysis needs to be undertaken to understand the nuances and variety that exists among Latinos in their voting preference and participation (or lack thereof, as we see in the Bronx).

Again, I note that there is a certain correlation between Caribbean and non-Carribean Latino voters and candidate support by borough. While there are South and Central American voters in all parts of the city (just as there are other Latino groups that are more spread out than in past decades), there is a larger concentration in Queens, hence the larger share of Mamdani support there.

Furthermore, Latino voters in Queens are not as unfamiliar with progressive candidates as voters in other boroughs. Let us not forget that Alexandria Ocasio-Cortez, who like Mamdani, is a Democratic Socialist, represents chunks of Latino-majority sections of Queens, and that Queens is also the place where progressives like Catalina Cruz, Jessica Gonzalez-Rojas, and Jessica Ramos have been elected.

I realize that some may not categorize Ramos as a progressive in light of her endorsement of Andrew Cuomo; yet I believe her voting record would certainly make the case for her affinity with progressive values. Though she is Latina, I did not include State Sen. Kristen Gonzalez, another Queens Latina elected official, since she does not represent a Latino-plurality district, at least when it comes to the voting population. Gonzalez is also a Democratic Socialist.

Another theory of mine is that although Queens Latinos, particularly in East Elmhurst, Corona, and Jackson Heights, now have about a 25-year solid voting presence. Historically speaking, they can still be considered fairly new voters and less influenced by machine-backed political maneuverings, at least compared to Latino voters in Manhattan and the Bronx—mostly Caribbean voters—who have been voting for well over half a century.

And it is only within the last decade and a half or so that there have been enough Latino voters to change political representation within their respective neighborhoods from non-Latino to Latino. Interestingly, the first Latino to win elected office in the history of Queens was Hiram Monserrate in 2001.

I must note that these advancements in representation were made by sheer determination, and often against the wishes of the Queens Democratic machinery. This is a very important detail that must be included in any analysis of the Latino political reality in Queens. Compared to the Bronx, there is no real history of Latino voter engagement from the Queens Democratic County organization, and no real effort to increase Latino political representation in a borough that continues to see an increase in the Latino general and voting population.

In this sense, one can say that although there are a number of Latino elected officials in Queens, none can technically be considered "machine" or "establishment" candidates, perhaps with the exception of term-limited Councilman Francisco Moya.

The Bronx political reality presents a stark contrast to Queens. After many years of truly revolutionary movements by a number of Puerto Rican leaders, Latinos battled their way to the top of the Bronx Democratic apparatus. Nothing was handed to these Latinos, who simply sought a voice in the political process. They fought for and earned proper political representation.

After decades of struggle, Latinos began to win elected office, eventually becoming the heads of the Bronx Democratic organization, and earning the Bronx borough presidencies. (At this moment, Latinos no longer have any boroughwide representation, nor do they hold the chair of the Bronx Democratic organization, though the Bronx is the only Latino-majority borough.)

After some time, Latinos in the Bronx no longer were the reformers (as they once were called), and in many ways lost the revolutionary edge that earned them representation. Many Latinos became, and continue to be, part of the establishment. In turn, many of the voting patterns among Latino voters in the borough tilted in that direction.

This continues to be the case, and in my view, partly explains why Cuomo beat Mamdani in the Bronx in the primary, and why Mamdani is receiving less support from Latinos there compared to other boroughs. There seems to be a long-held affinity to machine-backed candidates, though there are some rare exceptions.

The differences may also be influenced by age. Based on my own analysis of several voting data sources, I observe that Puerto Rican voters, for instance, tend to be older than other Latino groups, like Ecuadorian and Colombian voters. Cuomo seems to have received his largest share of support from Puerto Rican seniors than from any other Latino subgroup (though again, Mamdani still wins a plurality of this vote). Part of this reality may also be explained by Cuomo's strong name recognition among older voters, particularly those who also have memories of Mario Cuomo, the former governor and Andrew Cuomo's father.

The HF poll, coupled with the most recent election results, has given us much to explore, analyze, and ruminate on with respect to the complicated "Latino vote." The forthcoming general election will certainly shed more light.

An Excursus

39

Debunking Myths about Latino Vote Involves Examining Religious Ideologies

Our POLITICAL DISCOURSE IS replete with myths. Contrary to religious myths, the political kind are often riddled with meaningless and baseless claims that have little or no foundation in truth. Two of the more recent myths espoused by many political voices across the nation is that Latinos are either leaving the Democratic party in droves, or that Latino independent voters are voting for Republican candidates in overwhelming numbers. Such myths must be debunked—though with some nuance.

What drove the myth of a supposed widespread Latino "defection" was largely exit polling during the 2020 presidential election. Some of these exit polls showed heavy swings in traditional Democratic-leaning Latino areas, leading some observers to speak of a realignment in Latino politics in America. While this specific myth is occasionally true (like in Miami-Dade County in Florida, a geographic area with a large number of Latino Democratic voters), the larger truth is that several state-by-state analyses and studies undertaken by credible entities, like Equis Research and the UCLA Latino Policy Initiative, have demonstrated that Latinos did, in fact, overwhelmingly vote for now President Joe Biden, with Biden beating Trump in some key states by a margin of 3 to 1.

What drives the discrepancies that exist between exit polling data and the Equis and UCLA type of studies are that the former tends to rely on samples that do not contain sufficient Latino voter responses, making the data wholly unreliable, while the latter studies the actual election results, with the use of ethnic modeling data from state voter files. In short, the types of analyses that Equis and UCLA undertake are more accurate and prove that the notion of a Latino defection is an idea largely blown out of proportion by the mainstream press and others whose own agendas drive such false narratives.

The 2022 midterm elections continue to demonstrate the falsehood of the Latino defection myth. Here is what preliminary results indicate. In Arizona, Latino support for the Democratic (and incumbent) Senate candidate, Mark Kelly, remained steady in the high 70-percent mark. Republicans did not improve on Trump's 2020 performance in high Latino precincts. In Nevada, Latinos proved to be a key bloc in Senator Catherine Cortez-Masto's re-election efforts. She received almost 70 percent of the Latino vote. Both Arizona and Nevada were critical for Democrats in their battle to retain control of the Senate, and Latinos delivered for them.

In Pennsylvania, Latinos voted for Democratic candidates for governor and senate in large numbers, giving them close to 80 percent of their support. Democratic candidates in Wisconsin also received the lion's share of the Latino vote. Interestingly enough, in South Texas, a place where we did observe a certain swing among Latinos moving from solidly Democrat to support for Donald Trump and other Republicans in 2020, this time we saw no gains for Republicans.[1] Latinos supported Beto O'Rourke in higher numbers than Republican Governor Greg Abbott, and the three Republican candidates for Congress lost their races handily.

These numbers notwithstanding, there are indeed some locations where Latinos have trended more Republican, and this is where the debunking of the myth of a Latino defection requires some nuance. The most obvious such place is Florida, and more specifically Miami-Dade. The realities of Latino voting patterns in Florida prove that the notion of *a* single Latino vote is quite complex. Much has been said about the non-homogeneity of Latinos, and that is certainly true. Latinos come from a variety of Latin American countries, with differences in culture, language accents, histories, and the like. These differences are also evident in the voting behavior of some Latinos, voting patterns that are driven by a variety of ideological positions. And it is my contention that, contrary to the conventional thinking

1. https://rollcall.com/2022/11/17/gop-fell-short-in-latino-heavy-areas-along-u-s-mexico-border/

of many political scientists and other political observers, these ideological differences are largely driven by religious leanings, not economic ones.

Again, let's look at Florida. A majority of Latino voters there voted for the Republican candidates, Governor Ron DeSantis and Senator Marco Rubio. Carlos Odio from Equis Research has observed[2] that this is the first time since 2006 that Republicans have won a majority of the Latino vote in the Sunshine State. Yet again the Florida context points to the diversity within Latino communities. Republican candidates won by large margins in heavy Cuban precincts. Outside of Cuban-majority precincts, Republicans did not fare as well, losing most of Latino-majority precincts in counties in the Central Florida area. These counties now have a high number of Puerto Rican voters. Yet Odio observes that even these counties have experienced a decline in Democratic support. Clearly, there is no one-size-fits-all reality to understanding *the* Latino vote.

I conclude with a confession regarding some myths about the Latino vote. My hunch is that there is an element of the myth of Latinos as a type of swing vote that Latinos themselves have intentionally not debunked, despite the fact that Latinos have historically voted for Democratic candidates in larger numbers than Republicans, and as we continued to see in the 2022 midterm elections. Part of this resistance to myth-debunking may come from a place of defiant self-importance. Self-importance has been something that Latinos have had to grab for themselves, for others have ignored their plight for so long. In part for this reason early political figures like the Mexican Edward Roybal and the Puerto Rican Herman Badillo joined forces to create the notion of a uniform Latino vote. They realized that despite the variety that exists among Latin Americans in the US, there was much that united them. This also made practical political sense to them, as both leaders saw the potential to obtain long-denied power for their people through the concept of a pan-Latino identity.

This mission to create a sense of a pan-Latino reality was in some ways a rallying cry that declared that Latinos were *el futuro* (the future). The increase in Latin American descendants in the US could not be ignored, though for all practical purposes it was. Roybal's and Badillo's efforts would not produce the fruits they hoped to see, but the demand for respect had been made.

In some ways, the denial of this myth-debunking is also a rallying cry of sorts. It is the cry of Latinos that we are no longer *el futuro*, but rather

2. https://x.com/carlosodio/status/1594734864376516608

estamos aqui (we are here). While Roybal's and Badillo's fight was one for recognition, the rallying cry today is one for respect. It is undeniable that both national parties, but perhaps more so the Democratic party—a party to which Latinos have largely remained faithful—have taken them for granted. This unfortunate reality can be seen in several ways, from lack of investment in Latino communities to the denial of proper Latino political representation. With that in mind, could it be that the idea of Latinos as a quintessential swing voting bloc is one that Latinos themselves prefer not to debunk in order for the national political parties finally to take their plight (and vote) seriously, as well as their clamor for proper representation?

40

Moving Beyond Babylon
Latino/a Evangelicalism and Pentecostalism's Struggle for Ecclesial and Political Liberation

THE THEOLOGICAL, CULTURAL, AND political shifts evidenced in Latino Evangelicalism and Pentecostalism are among the most dramatic changes in recent US American Christianity. This ecclesial tradition was once unique for its prophetic utterances from the pulpit, as well as its distinctive musical rhythms and sounds. Formerly known for its preference for hymnals and acoustic pianos, its culture shifted and Latinos/as now sprinkle their music, liturgy, and sermonic stylings with the *sazón* of their own culture. Pianos gave way to the *guitarras, congas,* maracas and *güiros. Coritos* (short hymns) took the place of hymnals, and quickly *No Hay Dios Tan Grande Como Tu,* expressed in the rhythmic pulsation of the *clave I* or *clave II,* replaced the grand old hymn *How Great Thou Art.*

Both the sermons and the *coritos* were a clear contrast to the ways in which their Anglo evangelizers had taught Latinos/as to "do church." Now, the Latino/a Evangelical and Pentecostal tradition is more or less a carbon copy of its White counterpart, evidenced by the mimicking of the now stale rock-inspired musicality, the pop-psychology-type sermons, and the altars turned musical stages. In addition to adopting a caricature of White Evangelical liturgical and homiletical practices, Latino/a Evangelicals have also embraced the often intertwined cultural and political idiosyncrasies of their White counterparts, as we saw most recently in their support of conspiracy theories behind the COVID-19 pandemic and their ridiculing of states' mask policies.

We see this wholesale adoption of White Evangelical practices in the Latino/a Evangelicals' increasing support of the White nationalist philosophy which undergirds the White Evangelical theological position. The 2016 presidential election, Trump's subsequent term in office, and the 2020 presidential election have made this all much more publicly clear. According to research undertaken by Claremont McKenna religious studies professor Gastón Espinosa one month before the election, more Latino/a Evangelicals supported Trump than Biden, the *only group* among Latino/a Christians whose voting preference tilted toward Trump. In fact, the poll showed 48% of Latino Evangelicals supporting Trump for re-election. Biden led Trump among Latino/a Catholics and Latino/a Protestants. The Latino/a Evangelical vote was something Trump coveted, creating along the way the "Evangelicals for Trump" movement and receiving the endorsement of Miami megachurch pastor Guillermo Maldonado. While further research in light of the actual election results is still ongoing, it is quite possible that Trump's victory in Florida, for instance, was in many ways made possible by a large swath of Latino/a Evangelical voters. Espinosa's poll showed not only that Trump was increasing in favor among this bloc, but also that Latino/a Evangelical voters would potentially increase Trump's share of the Latino/a vote overall and hence increase his likelihood of victory in the Sunshine State.

The quantifiable evidence of the Latino/a Evangelical and Pentecostal embrace of White Evangelical theology and culture has been tracked by Janelle Wong's excellent work, *Immigrants, Evangelicals, and Politics in an Age of Demographic Change*. There Wong notes that Latino/a Evangelicals tend to share more of the conservative ideology of White Evangelicals than their Black counterparts, including its support of Trump. Wong's study, undertaken a year after the 2016 election, noted that a third of Latino/a Evangelicals supported Trump. Hence, if Espinosa's pre-November 2020 poll is accurate, and his past polls would suggest that this one is, Latino/a Evangelical and Pentecostal support for Trump increased by a whopping 18% in four years!

Latino/a Evangelical and Pentecostal voter preference is a manifestation of the socially conservative ideology espoused by their White counterparts. As Wong explained, Latino/a Evangelicals share with Whites a disdain for the LGBTQ community, overwhelmingly support for a ban on same-sex marriage, the legalization of abortions, support for the death penalty, and other social issues. Wong did notice some deviations between Latinos and Whites when it came to economic issues, like taxing the rich and government-sponsored universal health care, with Latino/a Evangelicals tending to support those issues in larger numbers than their White counterparts.

Interestingly, Black Pentecostals and Evangelicals have followed a different track from Latinos/as. Blacks, for the most part, have resisted the capitulation to White Evangelicalism and Pentecostalism that is so evident among Latinos/as. Across a myriad of social issues and voter preferences, Blacks have been historically consistent in their postulations, and have tended to resist the political and social ideologies of Whites more than their Latino/a neighbors. This is something Wong has likewise noted in her work. Not that Black Pentecostals and Evangelicals are thoroughly progressive in their social and political leanings, but they have been less rigid in their own conservatism than Latinos/as. This can be seen, for instance, in their vote preference for Joe Biden in 2020. In a survey conducted by Pew Research, 90% of Black Protestants preferred Biden over Trump.

I submit that Latino/a Evangelicals and Pentecostals must be more like their Black brothers and sisters. And I say this knowing that while key differences exist in the plight of both oppressed groups, Blacks and Latinos/as share many similar struggles, including cultural and racial oppression and economic injustice. Yet, why then have we Latinos/as been more willing to capitulate to White theology and culture, rather than stand alongside our Black brothers and sisters?

While the response to this query is wide-ranging and indeed complicated, the legacy and psychological trauma of colonialism and conquest among Latinos/as runs deep and continues to shape our theology, ecclesial practices, and political and social leanings. Furthermore, the eventual indigenization of Black Christianity has a longer history in the U.S. than Latinos/as Christian expressions. Latino/a Evangelicalism and Pentecostalism arose only in the twentieth century, a direct result of aggressive and deliberate White Evangelical and Pentecostal evangelistic efforts. Thus, Latino/a Evangelicalism and Pentecostalism are a direct product and offspring of their White counterparts. And while indigenous efforts did take place within the Latino/a Evangelical and Pentecostal church, recent practices have catapulted them back to their parental conception, though now with new twists and theological and cultural turns.

Clearly there are other theories behind this Latino/a capitulation. But the fact remains that Latino/a Evangelicals and Pentecostals have chosen the path back to captivity; they have returned to Babylon.

Latino Evangelical leaders warrant the brunt of a necessary castigation for leading astray Latino/a Evangelical and Pentecostal adherents. They have led their people in deviating from the prophetic roots of the Latino Evangelical and Pentecostal theological and ecclesial traditions, prophetic roots that were strong enough to counter the ecclesial and political powers and denounce injustice in the name of the Gospel. Instead, they have capitulated to the agenda of White Evangelicalism and Pentecostalism, an agenda that denigrates the understanding of the human being as the *imago dei* and instead has sold the Gospel truth of liberation to sustain political power and influence. Latino Evangelical and Pentecostal leaders' capitulation to the agenda of White Evangelicalism has resulted in them being content with the scraps and crumbs, the leftovers of what their White counterparts' feast. Those scraps and crumbs take the form of having their picture taken praying or eating with the President of the United States, and having coffee with those in political and ecclesial power. Has the dynamic, earth-shaking engagement for which Latino/a Evangelicalism and Pentecostalism was once known lost its bite, its leaders now content with political and ecclesial porridge?

Latino Evangelical leaders are leading their followers into a modern-day lion's den. The tradition needs modern-day Daniels willing to grab and muzzle the lion, not the cowardly acts of those willing and eager to bow down to the Nebuchadnezzars of the world. Only in this way can the Latino Evangelical and Pentecostal church become again a locus of survival and struggle against the injustices that continue to denigrate, delimit, and kill.

It is not too late for Latino/a Evangelicals and Pentecostals to retrieve their prophetic legacy. If they have the courage to do so, they will again be able to embody in word and deed the liberative power of the Good News they profess.

Bibliography

AnaMariaForNY.com. "Endorsements." https://www.anamariaforny.com/endorsements.

Archila, Ana Maria. "The Question Isn't Whether Antonio Delgado is Latino, It's Whether He'll Stand Up For Our Community." *Gotham Gazette*, May 19, 2022. https://www. gothamgazette.com/130-opinion/11308-is-antonio-delgado-latino-stand-up-ommunity-lt-gov.

Baretto, Matt, et al. "eiCompare: Comparing Ecological Inference Estimates across EI and EI:RxC." *The R Journal* 8:2 (December 2016).

Barreto, Matt A., et al. "Metropolitan Latino Political Behavior: Voter Turnout and Candidate Preference in Los Angeles." *Journal of Human Affairs* 21:1 71–91.

Beltran, Cristina. *The Trouble with Unity: Latino Politics and the Creation of Identity*. New York: Oxford University Press, 2010.

Borges, Eddie. "Latinos Get the Shaft Again in Bill de Blasio's Three Cities." City & State New York, October 12, 2017. https://www.cityandstateny.com/opinion/2017/10/latinos-get-the-shaft-again-in-bill-de-blasios-three-cities/182355/.

Bragg, Chris, and Rebekah F. Ward. "Longshot Assembly Candidates Faced a Mogul's Millions." *Times Union*, May 16, 2022. https://www.timesunion.com/state/article/With-financier-s-1-5M-an-outside-group-knocked-17172084.php.

The Buffalo News. "Senate Confirms Rivera for Sate's Top Court Over GOP Objections." February 11, 2013. https://courts367.rssing.com/chan-6030509/all_p32.html.

Castillo, Marco. "Poverty in New York City: Social, Demographic and Spatial Characteristics, 1990–2019." November 16, 2022. https://academicworks.cuny.edu/clacls_pubs/110/.

Center for Brooklyn History Finding Aids. "Guide to the Antonia Denis Collection." https://findingaids.library.nyu.edu/cbh/arms_1992_021_denis/.

City & State. "The 2022 Manhattan Power 100." City & State New York, August 15, 2022. https://www.cityandstateny.com/power-lists/2022/08/2022-manhattan-power-100/375648/.

Coltin, Jeff. "Endorsements in the 2022 Democratic Primary for Lieutenant Governor." City & State NY, June 22, 2022. https://www.cityandstateny.com/politics/2022/06/endorsements-2022-democratic-primary-lieutenant-governor/365733/.

Cook, Lauren, et al. "Congressman Ritchie Torres on NYC Shootings: 'Abandon' Defund the Police Movement, Invest in Social Infrastructure." PIX11.com, July 18, 2021. https://pix11.com/news/politics/pixonpolitics/congressman-ritchie-torres-on-nyc-shootings-abandon-defund-police-movement-invest-in-social-infrastructure/.

Dahl, Robert. "The Concept of Power." *Behavioral Sciences* 2 201–15.

Data for Progress. "Ritchie Torres is Popular With NY-15 Democratic Primary Voters in His District." March 11, 2022. https://www.dataforprogress.org/blog/2022/3/9/ritchie-torres-is-popular-with-ny-15-democratic-primary-voters-and-well-positioned-to-win-re-election.

DelgadoForNY.com. "Endorsements." https://delgadoforny.com/endorsements/.

Denis, Nelson A. "The Jones Act: The Law Strangling Puerto Rico." *New York Times*, September 25, 2017. https://www.nytimes.com/2017/09/25/opinion/hurricane-puerto-rico-jones-act.html.

Domínguez-Villegas, Rodrigo, et al. "Vote Choice of Latino Voters in the 2020 Presidential Election." UCLA Latino Policy & Politics Initiative, January 19, 2021. https://latino.ucla.edu/wp-content/uploads/2021/08/Election-2020-Report-1.19.pdf.

Francis-Fallon, Benjamin. *The Rise of the Latino Vote: A History*. Cambridge: Harvard University Press, 2019.

Frey, Kevin. "Torres Leads 120-Plus Lawmakers in Call to Shield Billions for Public Housing." NY1 Spectrum News, October 18, 2021. https://ny1.com/nyc/all-boroughs/news/2021/10/19/torres-leads-120—lawmakers-in-call-to-shield-billions-for-public-housing.

Gianaris, Michael. "Opinion: LaSalle's Rejection Was a Defeat for Albany Backroom Politics." *City & State New York*, January 23, 2023. https://www.cityandstateny.com/opinion/2023/01/opinion-lasalles-rejection-was-defeat-albany-backroom-politics/382061/.

Gotham Gazette. "Eli Valentin: Articles." https://www.gothamgazette.com/component/contact/contact/1492-eli-valentin?Itemid=327/.

Haslip-Viera, Gabriel. "The Evolution of the Latina/o Community in New York City: Early Seventeenth Century to the Present." In *Latinos in New York: Communities in Transition*. 2nd ed. Notre Dame: University of Notre Dame Press, 2017.

KathyHochul.com. "Endorsements." https://kathyhochul.com/endorsements.

Kelly, B. Rose. "Hispanics Face Racial Discrimination In New York City's Rental Housing Market." Princeton University, Woodrow Wilson School of Public and International Affairs, October 24, 2018. https://www.princeton.edu/news/2018/10/24/hispanics-face-racial-discrimination-new-york-citys-rental-housing-market.

Latham, Scott, et al. "Racial Disparities in Pre-K Quality: Evidence from New York City's Universal Pre-K Program." EdWorking Paper: 20–248. Retrieved from Annenberg Institute at Brown University. https://doi.org/10.26300/g1kf-9v58.

Lewis, Rebecca C. "Hochul Adds More Latinos to Her Administration." City & State New York, November 12, 2021. https://www.cityandstateny.com/politics/2021/11/hochul-adds-more-latinos-her-administration/186788/.

Louis, Errol. "A New Era for Latino Politics in New York?" New York Magazine Intelligencer, November 19, 2021. https://nymag.com/intelligencer/2021/11/a-new-era-for-latino-politics-in-new-york.html.

———. *You Decide with Errol Louis*. Podcast. https://podcasts.apple.com/us/podcast/eli-valentin-new-yorks-new-latino-population/id1448438816?i=1000542273859.

Lynn, Frank. "Bronx Minority Democrats Given Aid." *New York Times*, August 3, 1982, B3. https://www.nytimes.com/1982/08/03/nyregion/bronx-minority-democrats-given-aid.html.

The Marist Poll. Marist Poll of 1,117 New York Registered Voters. Conducted October 3–6, 2022. https://maristpoll.marist.edu/wp-content/uploads/2022/10/Marist-Poll_NY-NOS-and-Tables_202210101405.pdf.

Mearsheimer, John. *The Great Delusion: Liberal Dreams and Intentional Realities*. New Haven: Yale University Press, 2018.

Meyer, David. "Rep. Ritchie Torres Declares 'Defund the Police' Dead in NYC." *New York Post*, February 3, 2022. https://nypost.com/2022/02/03/rep-ritchie-torres-declares-defund-the-police-dead-in-nyc/.

Molina, Alejandro. "Latino Evangelicals Narrowly Favor Trump." *Christianity Today*, October 6, 2020. https://www.christianitytoday.com/2020/10/latino-evangelical-christian-voters-survey-trump-biden/.

Monyak, Suzanne. "GOP Fell Short in Latino-Heavy Areas Along U.S-Mexico Border." Roll Call, November 17, 2022. https://rollcall.com/2022/11/17/gop-fell-short-in-latino-heavy-areas-along-u-s-mexico-border/.

NALEO Education Fund. "2020 Census Profile New York." https://naleo.org/wp-content/uploads/2021/12/2020-Census-Profiles-NY.pdf.

———. "2021 National Directory of Latino Elected Officials." https://naleo.org/wp-content/uploads/2022/01/2021-National-Directory-Latino-Elected-Officials.pdf.

Odio, Carlos (@carlosodio). "Compare Crist (or Demings to previous Dem support in Miami-Dade: the worst under-performance is in the most Hispanic precincts. Early signs are that GOP gains were greatest among non-Cuban, non-PR voters . . . the "LatAm" voters among whom Dems got 70% as recently as '16." X (formerly Twitter), November 21, 2022. https://x.com/carlosodio/status/1594734864376516608.

Ong, Paul M., et al. "COVID-19 Death and Vaccination Rates for Latinos in New York City." May 28, 2021.

Pastor, Néstor David. "Carlos Tapia, The Puerto Rican Luke Cage of the Brooklyn Waterfront." Centro Voices 11 (December 2018). https://centropr-archive.hunter.cuny.edu/centrovoices/chronicles/carlos-tapia-puerto-rican-luke-cage-brooklyn-waterfront.

Schlesinger, Arthur. *The Cycles of American History*. New York: Houghton Mifflin, 1986.

Siena College Research Institute. "October 28–November 1, 2018; 641 New York State Likely Voters." https://scri.siena.edu/wp-content/uploads/2018/11/SNY1018LV-Crosstabs_37042.pdf.

———. "Siena College Poll Conducted by the Siena College Research Institute; October 12–14, 2022; 707 Likely New York State Voters." https://scri.siena.edu/wp-content/uploads/2022/10/SNY1022LV-Crosstabs.pdf.

Skelding, Conor. "Police Reform Group Accuses Torres of Surrender on Right to Know." Politico, December 12, 2017. https://www.politico.com/states/new-york/city-hall/story/2017/12/12/police-reform-group-accuses-torres-of-surrender-on-right-to-know-143683.

Smith, Gregory A. "White Christians Continue to Favor Trump Over Biden, but Support has Slipped." Pew Research, October 13, 2020. https://www.pewresearch.org/short-reads/2020/10/13/white-christians-continue-to-favor-trump-over-biden-but-support-has-slipped/.

Soria, Chester. "Latino Group Slams De Blasio for 'Marginal Inclusion' in Appointment." Gotham Gazette, December 23, 2013. https://www.gothamgazette.com/index.php/transition/4787-latino-group-slams-de-blasio-for-marginal-inclusion-in-appointments.

Students First NY. "New York City Democratic Primary Poll." April 16–21, 2021. https://d3n8a8pro7vhmx.cloudfront.net/studentsfirstny/pages/5683/attachments/original/1619623039/StudentsFirstNY_Mayoral_Poll_Toplines_April_2021.pdf?1619623039.

SurveyUSA. "Results of SurveyUSA Election Poll #26585." October 19, 2022. https://www.surveyusa.com/client/PollReport.aspx?g=3b2816e1–9efc-4d5e-a219–3c3c9ab52993/.

Torres, Ritchie. "Puerto Rice is Not for Sale: Statehood Can Bring More Equality to the Island." *NY Daily News*, July 14, 2020. https://www.nydailynews.com/2020/07/14/puerto-rico-is-not-for-sale-statehood-can-bring-more-equality-to-the-island/.

Valentin, Elieser. "2020 Primaries: Winds of Change Shifting Latino Politics in New York City." Gotham Gazette. https://www.gothamgazette.com/columnists/other/130-opinion/9536–2020-primaries-latino-politics-new-york-city-ritchie-torres.

———. "A Closer Look at New York City Latino Voter Participation in the 2018 Elections." Gotham Gazette, May 24, 2019. https://www.gothamgazette.com/economy/130-opinion/8545-a-closer-look-at-new-york-city-latino-voter-participation-in-the-2018-elections.

———. "Commentary: Latinos in New York and the 2024 Presidential Election." City & State New York, December 22, 2024. https://www.cityandstateny.com/opinion/2024/12/commentary-latinos-new-york-and-2024-presidential-election/401837/.

———. "The Forgotten History of Latino Politics in New York." Gotham Gazette, July 25,2022. https://www.gothamgazette.com/130-opinion/11476-forgotten-history-latino-politics-new-york.

———. "The Future of Latino Politics in New York City." Gotham Gazette, May 17, 2017. https://www.gothamgazette.com/130-opinion/6937-the-future-of-latino-politics-in-new-york-city.

———. "Latino/a Religion and Politics." In *The Wiley Blackwell Companion to Latino/a Theology*, edited by Orlando O. Espin, 453–73. Malden: Wiley Blackwell, 2015.

———. "Latinos and the 2021 New York City Council Elections." Gotham Gazette, March 4, 2021. https://www.gothamgazette.com/130-opinion/10215-latinos-2021-new-york-city-council-elections.

———. "Latinos, Hochul, and the 2022 Election for New York Governor." Gotham Gazette, October 27, 2022. https://www.gothamgazette.com/130-opinion/11644-latinos-hochul-2022-election-new-york-governor.

———. "A Sad Day for Latinos in New York: Hector LaSalle's Rejection." Gotham Gazette, January 19, 2023. https://www.gothamgazette.com/130-opinion/11791-hector-lasalle-rejection-latinos-new-york.

Van Zuylen-Wood, Simon. "The End of Denial: How Trump's Rising Popularity in New York (and Everywhere Else) Exposed the Democratic Party's Break with Reality." *New York Magazine* Intelligencer, November 16, 2024. https://nymag.com/intelligencer/article/donald-trump-new-york-election-results-turning-red.html.

Velasquez, Josefa, and Clifford Michel. "NYC to Pick Up Two State Senate Seats Under Albany Redistricting Plan." The City, February 1, 2022. https://www.thecity.nyc/2022/02/01/nyc-state-senate-seats-albany-redistricting/.

www.ingramcontent.com/pod-product-compliance
Lightning Source LLC
Chambersburg PA
CBHW061740270326
41928CB00011B/2317